5806

Scharff, Robert, *ed.*
Yellowstone and Grand Teton National Parks, edited by Robert Scharff with the cooperation of the National Park Service. New York, D. McKay Co. [1966]

xi, 209 p. illus., maps (part fold.) 22 cm.

Bibliography: p. 200–202.

1. Yellowstone National Park. 2. Grand Teton National Park.
I. U. S. National Park Service. II. Title.

F722.S3   917.875   66–17872

YELLOWSTONE

and

GRAND TETON
NATIONAL PARKS

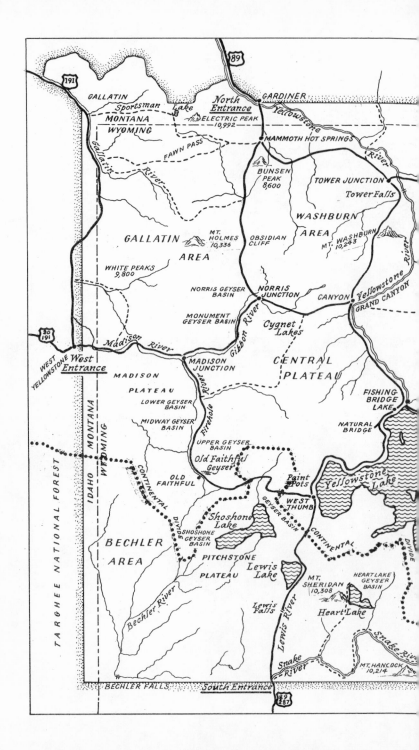

YELLOWSTONE NATIONAL PARK

IDAHO . WYOMING
MONTANA

COOKE
212

ALO
EAU

N. East Entrance

BARRONETTE
PK. 10,404

ABIATHAR PK.
10,928

ON PK.
800

DRUID PK.
9,583

BUFFALO
RANCH

MT. MORRIS
9,936

Old Gamekeeper
Cabin

THE NEEDLES
9,600

BISON River

MIGRATION

MIRROR

PLATEAU

PELICAN CONE
9,643

PARKER PK.
10,203

SADDLE MT.
10,670

HOODOO PK.
10,552

POLLUX PK.
11,067

SHOSHONE

MT. CHITTENDEN
10,189

NATIONAL

FOREST
East Entrance

AVALANCHE PK.
10,566

SHOSHONE
LODGE

16

ZLY PEAK
948

TOP NOTCH PK.
10,238

RESERVATION PK.
10,629

MT. LANGFORD
10,800

ARTHUR PK.
10,423

MT. DOANE
10,656

MT. STEVENSON
10,352

MT. HUMPHREYS
11,019

COULTER PK.
10,683

EAGLE PEAK
11,358

TABLE MT.
11,063

WO
CEAN
LATEAU

Yellowstone River

NATIONAL PARK BOUNDARY	
MAIN AUTO ROADS	
TRAILS	
STATE BOUNDARIES	

1 0 1 2 3 4
SCALE MILES

WITHDRAWN

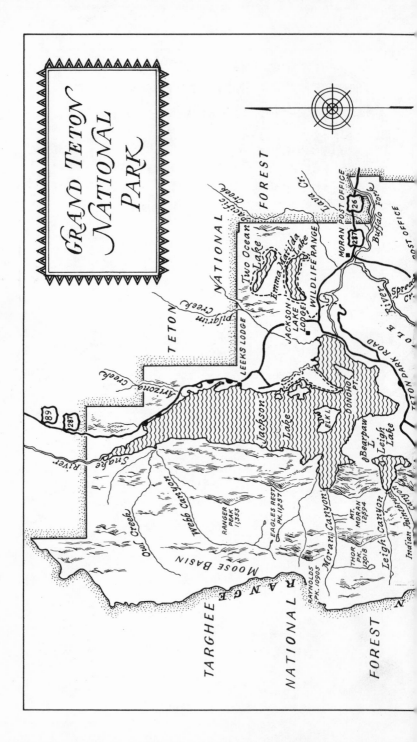

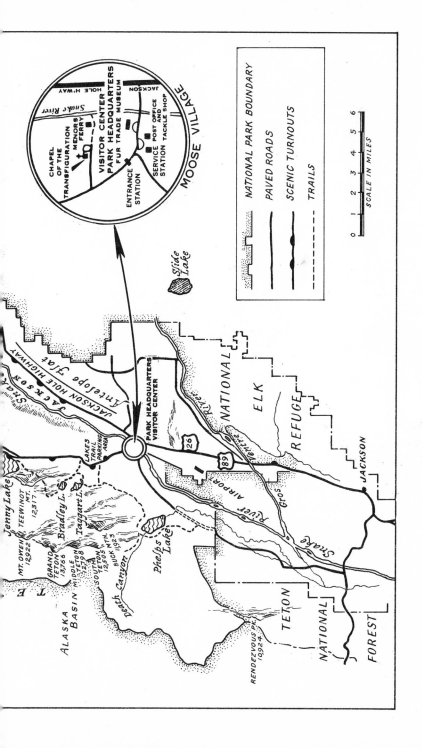

MOOSE VILLAGE

HOLE H'WAY

Snake River

JACKSON

CHAPEL OF THE TRANSFIGURATION

MENORS FERRY

VISITOR CENTER
PARK HEADQUARTERS
FUR TRADE MUSEUM

SERVICE POST OFFICE
STATION AND
TACKLE SHOP

ENTRANCE STATION

NATIONAL PARK BOUNDARY

PAVED ROADS

SCENIC TURNOUTS

TRAILS

SCALE IN MILES

0 1 2 3 4 5 6

Slide Lake

JACKSON HOLE HIGHWAY

Antelope Flat

Snake

PARK HEADQUARTERS
VISITOR CENTER

26

89

AIRPORT

Gros Ventre River

NATIONAL

ELK

REFUGE

JACKSON

Jenny Lake

LAKES TRAIL
PARKING AREA

MT. OWEN
12,922

TEEWINOT MT.
12,317

GRAND TETON
13,766

Bradley L.

MIDDLE TETON
12,798

Taggart L.

SOUTH TETON
12,505

BUCK MTN.
11,923

ALASKA BASIN

T E

Death Canyon

Phelps Lake

Snake River

TETON

NATIONAL

FOREST

RENDEZVOUS PK.
10,924

YELLOWSTONE

and

GRAND TETON

National Parks

★★

Edited by ROBERT SCHARFF
with the cooperation of the
NATIONAL PARK SERVICE

★★

DAVID McKAY COMPANY, INC.
NEW YORK

YELLOWSTONE AND GRAND TETON NATIONAL PARKS

LIBRARY OF CONGRESS CATALOG CARD NUMBER: 66-17872

foreword

YELLOWSTONE and Grand Teton National Parks are, in a very special sense, American heartlands. They reveal the full majesty and beauty of our country; the scope and reach of it, the awesome forces that have shaped it. The wildlife of the parks roams as an embodiment of America's natural vitality. There is a cleanness, a purity in these preserves that touches our highest ideals.

Lands like these have inspired America. Throughout our history we have shouted to mountains and laughed with rivers. We have marveled at the wonders of earth and the glory of its living creatures. We continue to do so here, on pleasuring grounds protected in trust for us and ours. Amid these splendid parkscapes we can fill our lungs and our eyes and our hearts.

STEWART L. UDALL
Secretary of the Interior

acknowledgments

To put a book like this together requires a great deal of help. And I certainly received it from the National Park Service and the concessioners at both Yellowstone and Grand Teton National Parks. Yellowstone's Chief Naturalist John M. Good and his assistant, Bryan Harry, and Grand Teton's Chief Naturalist Willard E. Dilley helped greatly in the gathering of material and checked both the manuscript and proofs for accuracy. In addition, I would like to thank Superintendent John S. McLaughlin and members of Yellowstone staff (past and present) such as James W. Godbolt, George D. Marler, Harold J. Brodrick, W. Scott Chapman, Jean Newhart, Robert Johnsson, William S. Keller, M. Meagher, and Aubrey L. Haines. I am indebted to Yellowstone Library and Museum Association for use of material and photographs. In Grand Teton National Park, Superintendent Fred C. Fagergren and the Grand Teton Natural History Association deserve special thanks.

Among the concessioners, Raymond C. Lillie of Grand Teton Lodge Company, Art Bazata, Norman E. York, Rolf Y. Olson and Pat Taylor of Yellowstone Park Company, and Isabel M. Haynes of Haynes, Inc., have been especially helpful in the preparation of the book. Frank Norris, Jr., and James R. Simon of the Wyoming Travel Commission, Richard V. Herre and Edwin C. Schaefer of Union Pacific Railroad Company, Roland Meyer of H. S. Crocker Company, Inc., James R. Graff of Sage Advertising Service, Inc., and Robert L. Adams of Needham & Grohmann, Inc., also have contributed greatly to the book's completion. Of all the people outside of the National Park Service personnel, however, Ronald R. Beaumont of the Yellowstone Park Company deserves special acknowledgment. He made all the arrangements and acted as coordinator of my research mission to the Parks. Thanks again to everyone who helped me with this book.

ROBERT SCHARFF

Contents

Chapter 1.

The Country of the
Yellowstone and Jackson Hole

WHILE neighboring Yellowstone and Grand Teton are man-aged by separate units of United States National Park Serv-ice, they have many things in common. With a scant 6½ miles be-tween these two great Parks, every visitor to this area should plan to see them both. In doing so, you will find the greatest geyser basins in the world, the largest mountain lake in North America, the most colorful of kaleidoscopic canyons, a fine array of wildlife, and one of the most spectacularly beautiful mountain ranges on the face of planet Earth. While these two Parks are tied together by topographic and geologic features of great scenic beauty, the Yellowstone-Grand Teton region had historical unity, too, especially during the early days of the Rocky Mountain fur trade.

MAN AND YELLOWSTONE

The first people to live in and around Yellowstone were, of course, the Indians. Of the three great tribes of this particular area—the Crows, the Blackfeet and the Shoshone—only a small, sub-tribe of the latter actually lived year-round in the present bounds of the Park. (The Shoshone have several sub-tribes and they were recognized and designated on a dietary basis, as "buf-falo-eaters," "deer-eaters," "salmon-eaters," "sheep-eaters" and "root-diggers." The Sheep-eaters inhabited the Gardner River

---

On facing page: *The Lower Falls of the Grand Canyon of the Yellowstone is perhaps the most breathtaking vista in Yellowstone National Park. The canyon has been eroded through rhyolite extensively decomposed by thermal gases. The Lower Falls is located at a point where the rock is practi-cally unaltered.*
Union Pacific Railroad Photo.

1

canyon area near Mammoth Hot Springs where the mountain-sheep hunting was good.) The other tribes, however, wandered in and out to hunt and fish. Burials unearthed by accident in 1941 and 1956 show that some eight hundred years ago there were Indian residents of what is now the busy Fishing Bridge campground.

For all practical purposes the Louisiana Purchase opened the way for American trappers to penetrate into the Rocky Mountain region, and they immediately took advantage of the opportunity. As the Lewis and Clark Expedition was descending the Missouri River in August of 1806, on the return to the United States, two trappers—Forest Hancock and Joseph Dixon—met the party while on their way to the Yellowstone River. John Colter, who had been a hunter for the expedition, asked permission to join the trappers and was allowed to do so. Thus, he turned back into the wilderness for another winter.

In the spring of 1807, as Colter again descended the Missouri River, he met the keelboats of the trader Manuel Lisa, who was then ascending the river for the purpose of establishing a trading post on the Yellowstone at the mouth of the Big Horn River. Colter was again induced to return to the mountains, and it was from "Manuel's fort" that he made the epic journey in the winter of 1807-08 through Pryor's Gap, past a thermal area (near present Cody, Wyoming), across the jumble of mountains into Jackson's Hole and probably across Teton Pass into the Teton Valley, from where he came northward up the Snake River into the present bounds of the Park, and from thence up the headwaters of the Snake to Shoshone Lake. He must have been surprised to find that large body of water at the source of the Snake, but when he crossed the Continental Divide eastward and discovered the beautiful Yellowstone Lake, his surprise must have been much greater, for he could not have suspected that so large a body of water would be found so high up on this mountainous plateau. But John Colter was to see still greater wonders, for he went down the Yellowstone River northward and discovered the Grand Canyon of the Yellowstone and its two majestic waterfalls. He gave an account of his strange travels when he returned to St. Louis three years later. His stories were not believed and a newspaper of that time humorously referred to the region of his travels as "Colter's Hell."

As time went by, other fur trappers undoubtedly came into this region, but none was so well-known as James Bridger. After the end of his three years' trapping stay in Yellowstone country, Bridger returned to St. Louis as Colter had done before him. He also told the stories of the wonders of the Park. He, too, was not believed, and his report of this incredible land was dismissed by newspaper editors as too "preposterous" to print. Up until this time Bridger had been a truthful man, but when he began to gain for himself the reputation of a liar, he thought he might as well earn it, and so he began to embroider just a little. He told about missing an elk with his rifle because a "pure glass mountain stood between us." (Today tourists stop and observe the black volcanic glass of Obsidian Cliff.) Bridger claimed an ice-cold spring at the top of a "lofty mountain gushed forth waters which raced downhill so fast that the river turned warm on the bottom." (Today, visitors can wade the Firehole River in certain places and feel the heat from the rocks underneath.) The waters of a creek near the Yellowstone River were so strong that they shrunk the horses' hooves. (Today, tourists who taste the waters of Alum Creek wear a puckered face long afterward.) Bridger told of an Indian Medicine Man who cursed the region with instant death. (Today, visitors admire the petrified trees along Specimen Ridge.) "And a fellow can catch fish in an icy river," drawled Bridger around evening campfires, "pull it into a boiling pool, and cook his fish without ever taking it off the hook." (Today, tourists photograph the hot springs that steam beside the trout-laden Firehole River.)

After Bridger and the other fur trappers, came some of the gold-seekers of 1849, who entered the Park, but finding no gold there, went on to California. In 1859 a small military expedition under the command of Captain W. F. Raynolds of the United States Army entered the northern section of the Park, but was not able to penetrate it very far because of the great depth of the snow. In fact, the snow is one reason why this area was not explored sooner. There are, in reality, only about four-and-one-half months of the entire year during which it is possible to move freely about in the *entire* Park. During the other months there is an average depth of between 4 and 14 feet of snow, and progress is impossible except by snowshoe, ski, and snowmobile. Other reasons were danger from the Indians, lack of interest in exploration except as it had to do with the discovery of gold, decline of the fur trade and the subsequent withdrawal of the trappers, and the Civil War, which gave the Government plenty to do in the East and discouraged any official explorations or geological surveys.

The second most important expedition in the history of the Park was the Cook-Folsom-Peterson Expedition of 1869. These three men were residents of the Territory, as it was then called, of Montana. They entered the Park and saw all the principal points of interest save the Upper Geyser Basin. They saw geysers and hot pools at other places in the Park, however, and returned to Montana, where they told stories of the wonders that they had seen. Even as late as 1869 their stories were not believed, or at least were thought exaggerated.

The stories that they told, however, were sufficient to warrant the formation of the official exploring party of 1870. This was official only insofar as it was given a military escort, for it was composed of prominent Montana citizens who were influential enough to procure an escort consisting of Lieutenant Gustavus C. Doane and four enlisted men. The small party was made up largely of men who were persons of importance in the Territory, such as General Henry D. Washburn, surveyor-general of Montana, and Nathaniel P. Langford, who later was to serve as the first superintendent of Yellowstone National Park. The expedition has become known familiarly as the Washburn-Langford-Doane Expedition, and the memory of these three has been perpetuated further by the naming of mountains in their honor.

The party, in less than four weeks' travel through the Park, discovered and reported on most of the wonders John Colter may have seen more than sixty years earlier. Their only serious mishap occurred when one of their members, Truman C. Everts, became separated from the group and spent "thirty-seven days of peril" in the wilderness. He was found by another party and rejoined his companions in Montana long after they had left the Park. (He, too, has a mountain named for him.) During their sojourn in the area and after having given up their search for Everts, the group stumbled upon the Upper Geyser Basin and stopped for a day to marvel at and name Old Faithful.

Then, despondent over the loss of their companion, they pressed toward home. Near the end of their journey, they camped where the Firehole and Gibbon Rivers come together, at what is now Madison Junction, under the shadow of National Park Mountain. Around a campfire on the night of September 19, they discussed possibilities of exploiting Yellowstone. They suggested dividing the area among themselves, because they knew that people in years to come would gladly pay to see the wonders of this land. Finally, Cornelius Hedges, a Montana judge, spoke up. He thought that there should be no private ownership of any part of the region, but that it should be set aside as a great park to be protected in its natural state for the use and enjoyment of all people.

The suggestion fired their imaginations, and they talked far into the night, trying to devise a way to protect this land from the westward movement of civilization that could destroy its beauty. On December 18, 1871, William Clagett, a newly elected member of Congress from Montana, introduced a bill for a National Park Act in the House of Representatives. The bill was passed on January

On facing page: *Yellowstone Lake as viewed from Lake Butte.*
Union Pacific Railroad Photo.

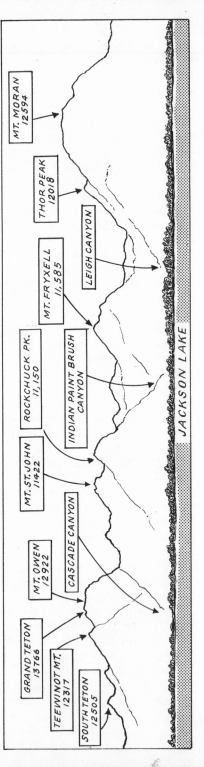

MT. MORAN 12594

THOR PEAK 12018

MT. FRYXELL 11,585

LEIGH CANYON

ROCKCHUCK PK. 11,150

MT. ST. JOHN 11422

INDIAN PAINT BRUSH CANYON

MT. OWEN 12922

CASCADE CANYON

GRAND TETON 13766

TEEWINOT MT. 12317

SOUTH TETON 12505

JACKSON LAKE

30, 1872. Clagett personally took the bill to the Senate, where it was passed on February 27. On March 1, President Ulysses S. Grant signed the bill which created Yellowstone National Park—first in the Nation, first in the world.

The idea of a Federal reservation of an area with park values was not entirely new, however. As early as 1790 the parks in Washington, D. C., were established for the enjoyment of the city's residents and visitors. In 1832, Congress established the Hot Springs Reservation in Arkansas "for the future disposal of the United States, and [it] shall not be entered, located, or appropriated, for any other purpose whatever." This reservation is now a National Park. And in 1864 the Federal Government granted Yosemite Valley and the Mariposa Grove of Big Trees to the State of California for park purposes. Later, this area, too, became a National Park. But the concept of setting aside a place of extraordinary character and national significance as a National Park for the benefit and enjoyment of all the people was first put into practice with the establishment of Yellowstone.

Five civilian superintendents saw the park through its important beginnings. In 1877, Nez Percé Indians, led by Chief Joseph, passed through Yellowstone during a retreat after they were routed in a series of continuing battles through the summer, in which three hundred lives were lost. In 1886, administration of the park was turned over to the U. S. Army. In 1894, a law was passed (Lacey Act) "to protect the birds and animals in Yellowstone National Park, and to punish crimes in said park." Not until the Lacey Act, which carried heavy penalties for poaching wild game, became effective did all hunting in the Park finally stop. On August 25, 1916, President Woodrow Wilson signed the act of Congress creating the National Park Service as a bureau of the Department of the Interior, and very shortly thereafter civilian superintendents were again appointed, replacing the military. Today, under the park superintendent, a staff of permanent and seasonal uniformed personnel provide service to protect the park and the visitor and to interpret and explain its natural features.

JACKSON HOLE AND THE GRAND TETON

Until shortly after 1800, Jackson Hole truly belonged to the Indians. Nothing was particularly outstanding about their history. This was primarily hunting country where parties of Crows,

On facing page: *Shoreline of Jackson Lake with the Teton Range as a backdrop. Diagram identifies major peaks with elevations.*
Union Pacific Railroad Photo.

Shoshone, and Bannock often summered. Evidences of their camps are common but there is no evidence to indicate that these were anything but summer hunting camps.

In 1807, the adventurous John Colter, whose name is linked closely with both Yellowstone and Grand Teton history, passed through the area on a solitary exploring trip, as mentioned previously. Within a few years many hunting and trapping parties of white men began to work through the region. It is believed that a group of French-Canadian trappers gave the mountains their name in 1819. As they saw these conspicuous peaks on the skyline from the west, they called them "Les Trois Tetons" (The Three Breasts). This romantic designation was readily adopted by the lonely trapping fraternity to whom the sharp snowy peaks (now known as Grand, Middle, and South Teton) became a beacon to guide them through the hostile wilderness.

One of the expeditions important in the early history of this country was that of the Astorians, who were in the employ of John Jacob Astor's American Fur Company. These trappers were sent to establish a trading post at the mouth of the Columbia River. For some reason, perhaps reports of hostile Indians, the group abandoned their boats and made their way across the Big Horn Mountains and up the Wind River. They detoured South hunting for buffalo, and crossed the Divide into the Hoback watershed, then down the Hoback into Jackson Hole. Leaving the valley by way of Teton Pass, they attempted to float the Snake and Columbia to the Pacific—a disastrous decision which almost cost the lives of the entire party. They called the Snake the "Mad River" after their desperate experiences in Hell's Canyon. Four men had been left in Jackson Hole to trap, but they were never seen again.

You will hear many references to the "mountain men" of Jackson Hole. They were hardy characters who, over a period of about two decades, in one way or another, contributed to the opening of the western frontier. In 1822, William Ashley and Andrew Henry formed the Rocky Mountain Fur Company and enlisted a hundred young men "to ascend the Missouri River to its source" on a trapping expedition. Among this group were Jim Bridger, James Clyman, Jed Smith, Thomas Fitzpatrick, Captain William Sublette, and David E. Jackson—destined collectively to become the greatest of the "mountain men."

By 1840 the fur trade was at an end, beaver hats (replaced by silk) having gone out of style. Jackson's Hole once more became the haunt of wildlife and an occasional Indian or trapper passing through. In 1860, Captain W. F. Raynolds of the Army Engineers (guided by Jim Bridger) led an expedition which passed through

Jackson Hole via Union and Teton Passes. Between 1875 and 1877, Dr. F. V. Hayden, of the U. S. Geological Survey, made two expeditions to Jackson Hole and Yellowstone. W. H. Jackson, expedition photographer, and Thomas Moran, the artist, accompanied the first expedition. Many landmarks were named for members of these expeditions—including Moran and St. John (both peaks), Bradley and Taggart, and Phelps (all lakes). These expeditions helped to make both the Tetons and the wonders of Yellowstone known to the world.

A few others visited the valley in these years. Hunters, occasional fishermen, a handful of die-hard trappers, and gold prospectors occasionally came. Jackson Hole has widespread placers of very fine gold. This gold originates in the conglomerate gravels forming Mount Leidy and Gravel Mountain but nowhere has it been found in paying quantities. During this time Jackson Hole acquired the reputation of being a desperado's hangout. This has been grossly exaggerated, for Jackson Hole was neither better nor worse than any other frontier town.

In 1884 the first settlers began to put down roots in this mountain valley, and the villages of Jackson and Wilson (just outside the Park) and, later, Moran (near Jackson Lake) were developed. Two old homesteads have been restored as historic buildings—the Menor's Ferry holdings, near Park headquarters, and the Cunningham place, on the east side of the valley. The latter is the site of a famous fray between a posse of men from Jackson Hole, from Idaho, and from Montana and two alleged horse thieves, who shot it out at daybreak there one April morning in 1893.

The Menor's (pronounced Meen'or) Ferry, originally constructed in 1892 by William D. Menor, was the principal means of crossing the Snake River in Jackson Hole for thirty-five years. It transported pioneers with teams, wagons, supplies, and livestock —horseback riders, hunters, trappers, fishermen, and prospectors from early spring until late autumn. Menor selected the site at the only location, he said, "Where the river is altogether in one place." When the first bridge was built at this site in 1927, the ferry was abandoned, but it was reconstructed in 1949. For the past several years the National Park Service has operated the ferry during the summer months, thus providing visitors to Grand Teton National Park an opportunity to enjoy the experience of a river crossing as it was made in pioneer times. Ferries of this type are rapidly disappearing from the American scene.

Grand Teton National Park was established and dedicated in 1929, but it included only mountains and a narrow strip of land with "piedmont" lakes. In 1950 it was enlarged by the addition of most of Jackson Hole National Monument, which had been

9

established in 1943. Included in the monument were some 52 square miles given to the United States by John D. Rockefeller, Jr., who had acquired and held the land in trust until the National Park Service could administer it. The gross area of Grand Teton National Park is now almost 500 square miles, of which about 98 per cent is in federal ownership. The Park is roughly rectangular, about 24 miles at its widest point and about 38 miles at its longest.

ADMINISTRATION OF THE PARKS

The Congress of the United States has placed the responsibility for administration of both Yellowstone and Grand Teton National Parks upon the Secretary of the Interior, who has delegated his responsibility to employees of the National Park Service, a bureau established in 1916. Affairs within each of the Parks are directed by a superintendent, assisted by personnel trained in the fields of protection, interpretation, maintenance, and administration, and their duties include most of the operations ordinarily performed by state, county, and local governments.

The superintendent in each Park is personally responsible for the establishment of broad policies and for the success of overall management, including maintenance of satisfactory public-service standards by private concessioners operating with the Park. This is done within National Park Service guidelines, and with the assistance of National Park Service staff specialists when necessary. The superintendent is assisted by an associate superintendent. While there are four major divisions in the Park operations—administration, maintenance, ranger services, and interpretation—the latter two are the ones a visitor usually meets.

PARK RANGERS

Uniformed park rangers are responsible for enforcement of rules and regulations in both Parks, fire detection and suppression, operation of entrance stations, and general supervision of activities in the several districts into which each Park is divided. They also handle lost and found property and receive suggestions and complaints from visitors.

If you are in any sort of difficulty or need information, see a Park ranger. He is there to help you. Remember, however, that he is also a Park police officer, commanding the same respect you give such an officer at home. He is authorized to issue summons for the violator of a Park regulation to appear before the U. S. Commissioner at Park headquarters. Persons who commit more serious offenses may be tried in the U. S. District Court at Cheyenne, Wyoming.

PARK INTERPRETIVE SERVICE

In both Yellowstone and Grand Teton, as in the other scenic areas of the National Park System, there is a varied interpretive program which will surely help you to greater knowledge and understanding of both the natural and the human history of the Parks. The program includes exhibits at the visitor centers, guided walks, campfire programs, informal talks, and accurate, easy-to-read literature. Specific details on the interpretive program are found in Chapters 3, 4, and 5. Remember that Park naturalists, who are also in uniform, are the Parks' interpretive force. They are here to help you understand what you see in the Parks, and they are responsible for all interpretive services, which are free of charge. The wise visitor plans to take part in some, if not all, of the naturalist activities.

HOW TO REACH THE PARKS

Yellowstone National Park—equal almost in size to Rhode Island and Delaware combined—is located partly in Idaho and Montana, but mostly in Wyoming. Grand Teton National Park is completely in the State of Wyoming. Both Parks can be reached by automobile, train, bus, or airplane. Bus, train, and airline schedule information is available from your local travel agent or from the Yellowstone Park Company or the Grand Teton Lodge Company (see pages 183 and 188 for addresses).

YELLOWSTONE NATIONAL PARK

By Automobile. Yellowstone can be reached from several transcontinental highways. Automobile associations, touring services, travel bureaus, chambers of commerce, and gasoline stations can furnish road information and maps. Inquiry should be made concerning road conditions and snow in high mountain passes in May and June and in September and October. Yellowstone is entered by road at five points:

From the North: Interstate 90, U. S. 10 and 89 via Gardiner, Montana.

From the West: U. S. 20 and 191 via West Yellowstone, Montana.

From the South: U. S. 26, 89, 187, and 287 via Grand Teton National Park and Jackson, Wyoming.

From the East: U. S. 14, 16 and 20 via Cody, Wyoming.

From the Northeast: Interstate 90, U. S. 10 and 89 via Silver Gate and Billings, Montana.

By Train. Yellowstone Park Company trains or buses of the Northern Pacific Railway at Gardiner and Silver Gate, Montana; of the Chicago, Burlington & Quincy Railroad at Cody, Wyoming; and of Union Pacific Railroad at Idaho Falls, Idaho.

By Bus. Yellowstone Park Company buses meet visitors at following locations and take them to all points within the Park:

North Entrance: Central Greyhound Lines to Livingston, Montana (connections to Gardiner).
West Entrance: Western Greyhound Lines to West Yellowstone, Montana.
South Entrance: Jackson, Wyoming and Jackson Lake Lodge.
East Entrance: Continental Trailways to Cody, Wyoming.
Northeast Entrance: Central Greyhound Lines to Billings, Montana (connections to Silver Gate).

By Airplane. Airlines serve the general areas surrounding the Park, but there are no airports within it. Scheduled service is available to the following airports and bus service to all points within the Park from locations marked with asterisk:

Billings, Montana (surface connections to Silver Gate*): Northwest Orient, Western, and Frontier Airlines.
Bozeman, Montana (surface connections to West Yellowstone*): Northwest Orient Airlines.
Cody*, Wyoming: Frontier Airlines.
West Yellowstone*, Montana: Western Airlines. This airline operates flights out of Los Angeles, California and Salt Lake City, Utah, connecting with flights from all parts of the United States.
Jackson, Wyoming (surface connections to Jackson Park Lodge*): Frontier Airlines.
Private aircraft generally arrive at either Jackson or West Yellowstone Airports.

GRAND TETON NATIONAL PARK

By Automobile. Grand Teton National Park can be reached by several important routes, and automobile associations, touring services, travel bureaus, and gasoline stations can furnish road information and maps.

From the East: U. S. 287 and 26 via Togwatee Pass.
From the Southeast: U. S. 187 and 189 via Hoback Canyon.
From the Southwest: U. S. 26 and 89 via the Snake River Canyon.

12

From the West: Wyoming 22 or Idaho 33 from U. S. 191 near Sugar City, Idaho. This brings you in over Teton Pass, a historic and spectacularly beautiful route. It is steep, however, and not recommended for trailer travel.

From the North: Via U. S. 89 and 287 from the South Entrance to Yellowstone National Park. This route is not open between November 1 and May 1.

By Railroad and Bus. The following rail and bus transportation is available to the Park:

From Idaho Falls, Idaho; Grand Teton Lodge Company buses meet and deliver passengers of Union Pacific trains.

From Rock Springs, Wyoming: By Jackson-Rock Springs Stages (bus) to Jackson.

From Yellowstone National Park: Daily bus service to Jackson Lake Lodge.

By Air. There is daily service into Jackson via Frontier Airlines from Salt Lake City, Utah; Riverton, Wyoming; Idaho Falls, Idaho Denver, Colorado and Billings, Montana. Frontier connects with other airlines in Denver, Colorado; Salt Lake City, Utah; and Billings, Montana. Grand Teton Lodge Company limousines meet all scheduled flights and transportation can be arranged for private flights.

Mileages from Locations in Grand Teton National Park to Points in Yellowstone National Park
From

Point in Yellowstone	Moose	Buffalo Entrance	Jackson Lake Junction
South Entrance	42	25	22
West Thumb	64	49	46
Old Faithful	81	61	58
Lake Junction	87	66	63
Madison Junction	96	82	79
Canyon Junction	102	88	85
Norris Junction	110	96	93
West Entrance	110	96	93
East Entrance	112	98	95
Tower Junction	121	107	104
Mammoth Hot Springs	132	118	115
North Entrance	137	123	120
Northeast Entrance	150	136	133

ENTRANCE FEES

Yellowstone and Grand Teton National Parks have been designated as recreation fee areas pursuant to the Land and Water Conservation Fund Act of 1965.

1. *Annual Recreation/Conservation Sticker*—This $7.00 permit admits the individual paying such fee and all those who accompany him in a private noncommercial automobile. This permit is good until March 31 of the year following issuance and admits the purchaser to all National Parks, National Forests, and other federal areas designated as "recreation fee areas."

2. *Daily and 30-Day Permits*—Shorter-period permits are available, but exact fees vary. For information inquire at Park entrance stations. All of the above permits are authorized by the Land and Water Conservation Fund Act of 1965. The Recreation/Conservation Sticker is a bargain for most families if they visit Grand Teton or Yellowstone more than once a year or if they intend to visit several federal areas.

Chapter 2.

Yellowstone—A World Apart

WITH so many natural phenomena within its 3,472 square miles (or approximately 2,221,766 acres), Yellowstone has often been called "a world apart." It is not difficult to see why. Within its several geyser basins, Yellowstone harbors more than ten thousand thermal features. About two hundred geysers, myriads of hot springs and bubbling mud volcanoes, and brilliant pools and terraces make it the most extensive and spectacular thermal area in the world. But Yellowstone is not alone the mighty surge of Old Faithful's periodic eruptions, the merry *plop, plop* of the paint-pots, nor the angry convulsions of the Black Dragons' Caldron. It is also the Grand Canyon of the Yellowstone River, 24 miles of twisting, sheer rock walls 1,200 feet deep, tinted with red and every shade of yellow visible to man—from the palest lemon to the most brilliant orange—given the decomposed rhyolite by various oxides of iron. It, too, is Yellowstone Lake, the largest mountain lake in North America at such high elevation. Yellowstone has many other natural phenomena to offer the visitor—as you will become aware as you read other chapters of this book—but for now let us take a look at its geological wonders.

GEOLOGICAL HISTORY OF YELLOWSTONE

To understand and appreciate the large number of natural curiosities which Nature has crowded into so small an area as Yellowstone, it is necessary that we know something of the geological history of this region. The earliest chapter of geology which we must consult is that which deals with the early times when this entire area was still sea-bound. At that time various forms of minute animal life formed calcareous shells generation after generation, age upon age, until the accumulations of the dead shells falling to the sea bottom had formed great layers of calcareous ooze. When eventually through the folding and buckling of the earth's crust the first rugged islands were lifted from the water and erosion carried down sand, silt, and sediment and made layers of land deposit upon the calcareous ooze, the latter was compresed into limestone. If you will look across the Gardner Valley to the bare, exposed east and northeast sides of Mount Everts, you will see these layers of sandstone and shale from the Age of Reptiles (period of dinosaurs). The fossils and other creatures of these sedimentary rocks indicate these strata were laid down in an ancient sea.

Omitting many chapters of geological history, we come to the time when this Rocky Mountain region was lifted from the sea waters by the folding and buckling of the earth's crust. The mountains in the Yellowstone region at that time must have been rugged and impressive, but they were not so high above sea as the present ranges. Trees and other plants preserved as fossils

Punch Bowl Spring: a delightful, ever-bubbling hot spring.
Union Pacific Railroad Photo.

indicate a moist, warm climate. As deformation and mountain-building proceeded, streams worked unceasingly to tear them down. However, the internal heat of the earth also seemed to increase locally and volcanic activity entered into the competitive program. Molten rock was injected into the cracks and fissures of the old sediments and lava poured out upon the surface.

The early part of this volcanic period was very violent. Explosions broke out in many places, hurling the overlying rocks aside and showering the land with fragmental rock from the depths, to cover it with breccias hundreds of feet thick. Quiet intervals were long enough to permit great forests to grow, only to be covered again by other breccias, tuffs, or sheets of lava. In the Yellowstone region the surface of the land never reached stability during the early part of the period. However, the first mountains were beveled down roughly and their stumps were buried beneath six to eight thousand feet of breccias and lava sheets.

At length volcanic activity of the violent sort subsided, and the rivers and streams attacked this great mound of volcanic debris, and proceeded to transport it to distant basins and flat areas. Some of it undoubtedly has helped to fill the gulf embayment and build the delta of the Mississippi. Eventually, the rivers and streams had succeeded in cutting deep valleys and sculpturing a rugged topography of greater relief than we have in the Yellowstone today.

But now a quiet type of volcanism challenged the persistent erosive powers of running water. Great fissures poured out lava in flow after flow until the valleys in the central area of the Park were filled to a depth of more than 1,000 feet with a rock called rhyolite. This rock occurs in a variety of forms from the soft friable material which easily grinds to a powder to that of the glassy structure so prominent in Obsidian Cliff. (The latter is essentially a mountain of volcanic glass—rhyolite that cooled so quickly, or was so viscous that it did not crystallize like most rock forms.) As a matter of fact, most of the rock formations you will normally see in the Park are rhyolite, though its varied forms might lead you to a different conclusion.

At the same time the old fissures which supplied the rhyolite were still steaming, the development of hot springs and geysers began as soon as the lavas cooled sufficiently to permit the temporary accumulation of water within their cracks and crevices. As time went on the hot water activity became more localized along the larger fissures. Most of these areas are now known as the geyser basins.

Throughout the entire period of volcanic activity in the region there were limited outpourings of basalt—another rock form. Though small in extent, compared with rhyolite, basalt is most important from a scenic point of view because it always assumes a form that attracts attention. The columnar palisades, near Tower Fall, in the lower canyon of the Yellowstone River is a fine example of basalt formations.

As time went by and the active volcanic period came to a close, other earth forces caused further uplift and deformation of the underlying rock through most of the Rocky Mountains. Colder seasons with more snowfall brought about the Great Ice Age. Now the streams in the higher regions had an ally in their work of tearing down the high places and filling up the low places. Great snow fields became so deep that their thicker portions turned to ice. Valleys were widened and deepened and mountain peaks and ridges were steepened and sharpened by glaciers which gnawed away at their flanks. The loosened rocks and sand were carried away in frozen rivers of ice. Then the ice melted and the debris which it contained was dropped, usually in a haphazard manner, to cover the ground here and there with patches of glacial drift. Capitol Hill in Mammoth is a good example of a glacial gravel or moraine. The gravel hills between Mammoth and Gardiner have been deposited by glaciers. At Canyon, near Inspiration Point, you will see the glacial boulder, a huge rock which rests on an andesitic lava flow. The only plausible explanation is that it was carried by a glacier, and it must have been transported several miles, because the nearest source of granite, of which it is composed, is some 20 miles off—a rather interesting evidence of glacial activity.

Since the end of the glacial periods, the Park's topography has changed relatively little. Today, it is generally described as a high mountain plateau with an average elevation of nearly 8,000 feet. As a matter of fact, it is really a series of several plateaus. The more important ones have been named and are known as Pitchstone, Madison, Central, Mirror, Solfatra, Two Ocean, and Blacktail Deer. Pitchstone Plateau is in the southern part of the Park and is situated between Snake River and headwaters of Bechler and Falls Rivers. Its mean elevation is 8,500 feet. Madison Plateau lies west of the Firehole Geyser basins at a mean elevation of 8,300 feet. The Central Plateau, with a mean elevation of 8,300 feet, is located between the Yellowstone and Madison Rivers. Mirror Plateau, at an elevation of 9,000 feet, is between the Yellowstone and Lamar Rivers. Solfatra Plateau is west of the Grand Canyon at an elevation of 8,000 feet. Two Ocean Plateau lies to the south of Yellowstone Lake and its mean elevation is 9,000 feet. Blacktail Deer Plateau is in the northern part of the Park, between the Yellowstone and Gardner Rivers. Its mean elevation is 7,500 feet. Actually, the Park's elevation ranges from about 5,000 feet near the north entrance at Gardiner to the 11,358-foot high Eagle Peak near the southern boundary. (*Note:* The valley, river, and canyon within the Park is spelled *Gardner*—after Johnson Gardner, an early trapper in the area—while the town just beyond the north entrance is *Gardiner*.)

Yellowstone Park lies in a central position of the Rocky Mountain System. In fact it has been referred to as the "heart of the Rocky Mountains." Abutting the Park on the north are the Beartooth and Snowy Ranges. Part of the Gallatin Mountains lie within the Park along the northern section of the western boundary. They are separated from the Snowy Range by the Yellowstone River. The Absaroka Mountains, so called from the Indian name of the Crow Nation, form the eastern boundary of the Park. They are very rugged in topography, affording no natural passes for their entire length.

The Teton Range lies south of the Park. It is not an extensive system, but one of great altitude and marvelous scenic beauty (see page 71). Lying wholly within the Park are two separate mountain masses known as the Red Mountains and the Washburn Range. The latter is situated between the Grand Canyon of the Yellowstone and the Gardner River. The most conspicuous peak of the range, as well as the most noted mountain of the Park, is Mount Washburn (elevation 10,243 feet). The Red Mountain Range is a small group of mountains between Heart and Lewis Lakes, southwest of Yellowstone Lake. Its principal summit is Mount Sheridan (elevation 10,308 feet).

The mountains of the Park as viewed, for example, from Mammoth give a geologic panorama which almost runs the gamut of geologic ages. Each mountain, ridge, or hill contains a different kind of rock and relates a separate chapter in the geologic development of Yellowstone Park. In the granite peaks of the Snowy Range to the north are some of the oldest rocks known, laid bare by erosion. Layers of sandstone and shale from the Age of Reptiles can be seen on the scarred face of Mt. Everts to the east and northeast. To the northwest are the rugged flanks of Sepulcher, consisting of ash and fragmental rocks thrown out of volcanoes by violent eruptions following the withdrawal of the ancient seas. In Clagett Butte due west of Mammoth, there is a hill of sedimentary rocks capped by a lava flow with a well-developed glacial cirque on its northeast side. A little farther south, Terrace Mountain consists of a lava flow overlaid by travertine, a hot springs deposit.

19

YELLOWSTONE HYDROTHERMAL FEATURES

The most unusual and unique of Yellowstone's varied topographic and geologic features are its hot springs and geysers. Millions of gallons of hot water bubble out of the earth each day in Yellowstone, and large volumes of scalding hot steam are emitted. Enough heat is given off in the Park to melt three tons of ice every second. All in all, one cannot deny that the earth under one's feet in Yellowstone must be very hot indeed. The geysers are dramatic but unusual evidence of the tremendous heat inside our world.

Although geysers are quite rare, other signs of the great heat of the earth are relatively common. Hot springs are found throughout the world. Volcanoes are active in many lands. Everywhere there is an increase in temperature downward. In most places the temperature increases a little more than 2° F. every 100 feet downward. Or in other words, in most places in the United States some 10 miles straight down the temperature is over 1,000° F. In Yellowstone the temperature increases much more rapidly than that. In the Upper Geyser Basin, a number of years ago, scientists drilled a bore hole. At 400 feet down, they recorded temperatures over 350° F. At this rate, temperatures would quickly rise above the melting point of rock itself only a short distance down.

HOT SPRINGS AND POOLS

Boiling springs are features of many volcanic regions. Long after dormancy of most volcanoes, fumaroles and boiling springs are found in and on their flanks, and sometimes in the surrounding country at a distance of several miles from the volcano's base. This early led to the theory that boiling springs and volcanoes are genetically related; that hot springs are one of the stages, the third and concluding stage, in volcanism.

While standing in one of Yellowstone's geyser basins, you can consider yourself floating on a rock raft over a pocket of red-hot molten material called magma. It is the magma, which is not too far below the earth's surface, that is the furnace heating Yellowstone's hydrothermal features. This magmatic furnace is banked with layers of volcanic (rhyolite) rock. Above this in the geyser basin are several hundred feet of sandy glacial gravel which forms the surface layer. This gravel is saturated with rain and snowmelt water. As this cold water filters through the hot ground and warms up, and since this water can return to the surface through fissures in the ground, all the conditions necessary for hot springs are met.

The names given many of the hot springs are suggestive of their fundamental distinction. Examples of those being designated as springs and pools are Morning Glory, Emerald, and Turquoise Pools, and Coral, Topaz, and Grant Prismatic Springs. The designation "pool" is arbitrarily applied. It does not, as some suppose, signify a non-flowing spring. All of the above-named pools, as well as the other "hot" ones, are in an overflow state most of the time.

In many of these pools and springs, the conditions are such that the water does not reach the boiling point, which is about 199° F. at the elevation of the Park. Most of the deep pools are of a beautiful blue color. Other pools seem to have all the colors of the spectrum moving about as through a revolving prism. Sometimes there is an iridescent effect similar to that of a film of oil upon water; but there is no oil here. There are also many beautiful hues seen in such pools as Black Sand Opal and Gentian Pools. There are doubtless many factors which cause these remarkable effects. First, there is a great depth of clear water which always presents a beautiful appearance. Second, there are the mineral deposits on the sides of the crater, producing indefinite reflection, the effects of which are multiplied by the refractive power of the water. In addition the mineral ingredients dissolved or suspended in the water doubtless add to the effect. But, the major cause is the growth of algae—a plant growth—that results in colors from yellow to green.

Algae vary in size from the very minute forms found in Yellowstone Park to seaweed forms whose stems resemble tree trunks and whose fronds rival the leaves of the palm in size. However, they do not have true stems, roots, or leaves. From the giant kelps of the oceans iodine and bromine may be obtained. Algae are used to some extent as a fertilizer, and there are many edible forms also.

The hot spring algae of Yellowstone are a wonder of life at high temperatures. Some can withstand temperatures up to 163° F. These are the pale green-yellow forms. As a rule the darker-colored algae live at low temperatures and the light-colored algae live at high temperatures. That is, the colors range according to the temperature, starting with pale yellow-green at the highest range. These forms grow more abundantly and deepen in color as the temperature drops, with reds, browns, and olive-browns appearing as the water cools even more. But, remember that not all of the natural colors about hot springs are algae. Some vivid colors are chemical deposits. Sulphur, iron oxide, and a few other deposits can be readily seen at such locations as Norris Geyser Basin.

There are some boiling springs, but these are usually of only secondary interest in comparison to the beautiful pools and springs. While they are generally just enormous caldrons, a few display peculiarities that are interesting. Some of them even show a geyseric tendency, in which the eruptive force is expended before it can produce any decisive result. Among the more important of these is Beryl Spring, in the Gibbon Canyon, which discharges a large volume of boiling-hot water. There are also several of these springs in the Norris and Firehole Geyser Basins. The odor which is so characteristic of many of the hot springs is due to a gas known as hydrogen sulfide.

Actually, hot springs are in a constant state of change; the change, however, is almost imperceptible except by comparison of records over decades. Earth movements cause abrupt changes. Before the Hebgen Earthquake in 1959, for instance, Leather Pool in the Lower Geyser Basin was a low-temperature "hot" pool. It received its name from leather-like brown algae that lined the bowl. Following the quake, the water temperature increased from 143° F. to boiling and killed the algae. The temperature still remains above the critical point for life. Thus, geologically speaking, hot springs are very fragile. Glacial gravel is unstable material, and in this basin the gravel is honeycombed by the sinuous roots of springs. The basin is particularly vulnerable to earthquakes. The jarring energy of a quake can make gravel bounce atop solid rock as does a marble on a wood floor that is hit by a hammer. As the gravel particles vibrate, their positions are readjusted. Compaction usually results and water displaced from around rock particles is forced to the surface carrying muddy material that clouds surface pools. Fractures accompany compaction and water levels in some springs drop as their discharge is diverted. Others increase in temperature as steam and hot water are directly led to them through newly opened fissures.

GEYSERS

A geyser is a special kind of hot spring from which water and steam are thrown to varying heights above the surrounding surface, at intervals that are usually irregular. They are natural hot-water fountains that play from time to time, emptying their channels of water and steam. The process requires from a few seconds, for the small ones, to as much as fifteen hours for some of the larger ones. The heights to which they eject the hot water varies from a few inches to as much as 250 feet. True geysers are *very* rare phenomena. Outside of Yellowstone—the world's greatest concentration of geysers—they are found only in Iceland, New

(*Continued on page 27.*)

The Yellowstone Geysers....

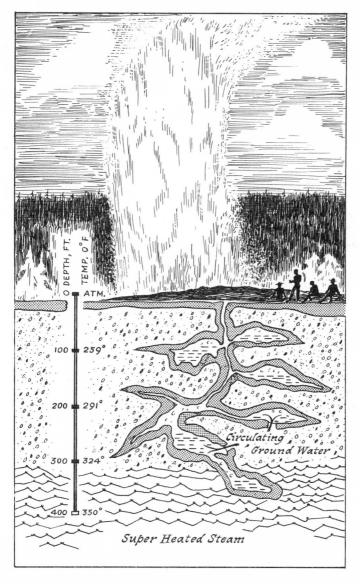

Scientists speculate that a geyser's underground plumbing system is generally as shown above. The depth and temperature data are from an actual test hole drilled in Yellowstone Park.

Geysers are of two main classes. Above the fountain-type, as illustrated by Grand Geyser in Yellowstone's Upper Geyser Basin. It shoots from 160 to 180 feet into the air, erupts steadily for periods varying from 15 minutes to 1½ hours at intervals of from 8 hours to several days. During quiet periods many fountain geysers look like colorful springs.

The second type of geyser, the cone-type, is illustrated by Castle Geyser, also in the Upper Geyser Basin at Yellowstone. This geyser erupts from the top of a cone, or mound, in a number of separate, spasmodic bursts, shooting from 30 to 60 feet high from 15 to 60 minutes at a time. Eruptions occur every 4 to 10 hours. Eruptive patterns vary for both types.

The most famous geyser of them all—Old Faithful. Contrary to opinion, this geyser does not *erupt once every hour. Intervals of eruption vary from 35 to 95 minutes, but have not failed in the eighty years the geyser has been observed. The geyser spouts from 100 to 185 feet high, and continues in play for from two to five minutes in spectacular display.*

Zealand, and the Kamchatka Peninsula in Russia. A few small geysers are found scattered in other parts of the earth. The only other natural geysers in the United States are those at Beowawe and Steamboat Springs, Nevada. Artificial geysers have resulted from drillings, such as those at Calistoga, California.

In comparison with a conventional hot spring, the "plumbing system" of a geyser is probably more intricate. The system has a delicate pressure/temperature balance that can be suddenly upset. A subterranean steam explosion is then triggered and water is driven upward. No one knows with *exact* certainty how a geyser works, for the obvious reason that no one has been inside during an eruption. However, by examining what can be seen, plus known scientific information, it is possible to come up with a plausible explanation.

It is safe to say that a geyser must have an available supply of water and heat, and a plumbing system strong enough to withstand a rather high steam pressure. Although the temperature in subterranean tubes, pipes, and chambers of the system is well above boiling, the water does not boil due to the pressure from the weight of the overlying water higher in the system. Roughly the same sort of thing happens in a pressure cooker on the kitchen stove. Put an open pot of water on the burner and before long, boiling begins with the liquid, water, changing into the gas, steam, which disappears into the air of the kitchen. But clamp a tight lid over the pot and the steam cannot escape. Since the confined space can hold only so much, soon no more water can turn into steam. The boiling stops even though the water gets hotter and hotter. The steam gets hotter, too, and if there were not a safety valve on the pressure cooker, the pot would explode. Now the confining water in the geyser's plumbing system is not so rigid as the top of a pressure cooker. When the water deep in the system gets hot enough, some steam does form. This expanding steam lifts the overlying water in the pipe leading to the surface. Thus, before the main eruption you will see some water come splashing out of the geyser. Usually most of this ejected water will fall back in the vent and the volume of water in the system will not be greatly changed. These false starts may occur a number of times but eventually enough water will be thrown out to reduce the weight of water in the vent pipe. The eruption is now triggered. With the confining pressure slightly relieved, the superheated water (a few degrees above boiling) down below flashes into steam, lifts more water out of the top, and generates more steam, and so on in a rapidly accelerating steam explosion. The explosion violently blasts the hot boiling mixture of water and steam high into the air through the nozzle-like vent.

27

The eruption ends when the superheated water is exhausted. If liquid water is exhausted first, a steam phase follows until the superheated water is spent. Refilling of the chambers ends the steam phase. Refilling can be abrupt, sometimes slow. A conventional hot spring has no confines that trap steam and so it escapes freely in fumaroles and boiling springs. It has been estimated that about 85 per cent of the water in geysers and hot springs has its origin as surface water from rain and snow. The water is returned to the surface by steam pressure after being heated in the geyser's subterranean plumbing system. The other 15 per cent of the water has its origin in condensed steam which was added from the hot gases rising from magma (the molten rock within the earth) at considerable depth.

The geysers are extremely variable in their eruptive patterns. No two geysers are alike, and to make for complication some geysers have more than one type of an eruption. Diverse as they are in behavior they can be put in two main classes. They are referred to as either fountain-type or cone-type geysers. In general the cone-type geyser erupts from the top of a cone or mound. At least one of the constricted parts of the tube is at the surface. During activity the water plays steadily for the entire duration of the water phase of the eruption. In the case of the fountain-type geyser the bowl or upper part of the crater is in the form of an inverted cone. During the quiet phase many of these geysers appear as colorful springs. During the eruption the water does not issue steadily, as in the case of the cone-type, but there are a number of separate, spasmodic bursts or explosions. The separate explosions, usually in fairly close sequence, make up the eruption.

Practically every factor pertaining to geyser activity is a variable one. Not only are there great variations in eruptive patterns, there are extreme variations in the length of the eruption intervals, of the quiet phases, also in the duration of the eruption. The intervals between eruptions for some geysers are less than a minute, and the duration, but a matter of seconds. Other geysers are known to have been in an active phase for over one hundred hours. The intervals for some geysers are a matter of days, weeks, months, or years. During an active phase some geysers discharge no more than a splash, while others discharge more than a million gallons. Some do a little of both. In the Norris Basin, for example, the major eruptions of Steamboat Geyser throw thousands of gallons of water 300 to 350 feet into the air on an irregular schedule, presently from seven to fourteen days. Steamboat returned from a fifty-year dormant state in 1961 and also has so-called ordinary eruptions in which water boils up two to three feet every three or four minutes.

No geyser is regular if regularity is defined as erupting at set periods. This includes Old Faithful. Contrary to popular opinion Old Faithful does *not* erupt every hour as regularly as clockwork. The *average* time between eruptions is about 65 minutes, but this is only a statistic. The actual interval may be as short as 35 minutes or as long as 95 minutes. But Old Faithful's reputation for dependability is well deserved. It has *never* missed an eruption during the more than eighty years it has been observed, and its variations follow a pattern that makes it reasonably predictable. That is, sometimes Old Faithful throws water over 180 feet in the air, other times only 100 feet. Old Faithful may continue to play for five minutes or it may stop after only two minutes. Since any eruption requires a certain amount of heat energy, the big long eruptions use more energy than the short ones. After a powerful eruption Old Faithful takes longer to recuperate; that is, for heat energy to build up in its underground system. The amount of water thrown out in an average eruption has been estimated at from 10,000 to 12,000 gallons, most of which runs into the Firehole River.

Detailed observations that have been made of the hot springs in the Firehole Geyser Basins have established the fact that the springs in most groups are connected subterraneously. Certain groups are also known to have underground connections with each other. All geysers that are known to be connected underground with other springs or geysers show great irregularity in their eruptive patterns. At indefinite, and sometimes long intervals, the thermal energy will shift its surface expression from one spring to another. On the other hand, not all geysers which show great irregularity are known to have underground connections with other springs. A few geysers, as Imperial and Excelsior, owe their great irregularity to alterations in underground structure.

New geysers do not occur often but, through the years, Yellowstone's thermal features may change characteristics, dying out or spouting with new vigor. The 1959 earthquake caused many changes, including 165 hot springs which suddenly became geysers. Hot springs and geysers in the Park are scattered over an area of 1,800 square miles.

FUMAROLES

As previously mentioned, fumaroles are the second phase of volcanism and exist where surface water is apparently lacking and where there is a vast quantity of superheated steam (a few degrees above boiling) generated far below. It has often been assumed that there has been an evolution from fumarole to geyser, that initially all were fumaroles. However, in the case of some springs their initial discharge is water. This happens as a result of mechanical fracturing of the ground which taps a zone of ground water. In areas where fumaroles occur they are generally associated with hot springs. The occurrence of fumaroles and hot springs together seems to be dependent upon the nature of the distribution of the ground water. Some springs seasonally change from fumarole to hot spring, the change being governed by available ground water.

The fumaroles which occur in areas where there is a scarcity of ground water frequently discharge superheated steam. This superheated state seems possible only if it is assumed that the steam originated in a magma, and that the ground through which the steam escaped was relatively dry. Below the zone of ground water in the thermal areas there would appear to be a zone of superheated steam reaching down to the magma. In some sections of the Park this zone reaches the surface, resulting in the superheated steam vents. Roaring Mountain has several powerful vents near the summit. See page 37.

MUD SPRINGS

A characteristic and interesting class of thermal phenomena is the mud springs that abound in all parts of the Park. They present an almost endless variety of form and aspect, but there are only two that need now detain us—the "paint-pots" and the eruptive springs, like Black Dragon's Caldron near Yellowstone River.

The paint-pots are caused by steam escaping from the heat source below the surface of the earth. The water is just sufficient in quantity to keep the mud or clay in a plastic condition, and the steam operates upon it precisely as it does upon a kettle of thick mush. Generally, there are various mineral ingredients, mostly oxides of iron, which impart different colors to different parts of the group. As the steam puffs up here and there from the thick mass, it forms the mud into a variety of configurations, frequently that of the lily. These configurations immediately sink back into the general mass, only to be formed anew by other puffs.

Mud springs, or paint-pots, are widely distributed in the Park. Some of the largest are found in the Mud Volcano Group, Norris Basin, West Thumb, Washburn Springs, and the Lower Basin. The odor of hydrogen sulfide is pronounced at these mud springs.

On facing page: *The Fountain Paint Pots, in the Lower Geyser Basin. Numerous mud springs, or paint pots, are found in this area and can be seen from a ½-mile-long Nature Trail.* Union Pacific Railroad Photo.

TRAVERTINE AND GEYSERITE

There are two rock-like materials that you will surely see while visiting hot springs and geysers. One is *travertine,* a calcium carbonate deposited by the hot springs at Mammoth, and the other is *geyserite,* a hydrous silicon dioxide, deposited wherever there are geysers.

The terraces of Mammoth Hot Springs are composed of travertine, which is a limestone formed by the precipitation of calcium carbonate from hot-spring waters. The hot waters moving from the lower strata towards the surface pass through layers of limestone and dissolve the lime, carrying it in solution to the surface. Carbon dioxide dissolved in the water aids materially in the process of solution. As the hot water reaches the surface the carbon dioxide escapes and the calcium carbonate in solution is precipitated as travertine, building up at a rapid rate the unusual terraced deposits that make Mammoth Hot Springs extraordinary among thermal springs of the world. Terrace Mountain is composed mainly of travertine. Glacial erratics rest upon its top, and a floor of travertine under Capitol Hill is taken as evidence of the pre-glacial origin of the thermal activity of these hot springs.

Looking about at the graceful terraces, you will note that most of them are in the shape of pans or steps, one above the other. This is due to the fact that hot water containing the lime in solution bubbles up out of the ground forming a pool. Naturally the water on the edge loses carbon dioxide faster than the water on the inside, so the carbonate is thrown out of solution and deposited faster around the outer edge of the pool. This keeps on until the water is almost walled off by this deposit. When the pool eventually fills up, it overflows and the water forms another pool down below it. The process is repeated giving the effect of pans or steps. From the margins of some springs a thin sheet of deposit, known as "hot-water ice," extends over some of the springs. It can be observed at the surface of still pools and forms rings and borders about others. After collecting as a thin crust it breaks away from the side and settles to the bottom.

On facing page: *Terraces of Mammoth Hot Springs rise in great stair-like tiers. Formed by travertine deposits, and colored by living algae, they continually build new basins. Mineral waters fill the basins, then cascade down to the ground.* Union Pacific Railroad Photo.

The coloring of the terraces is caused by Yellowstone's famous algae. The bleached white and gray areas indicate the dead portions of the travertine formations—that is, there are no active springs on it. The algae can only live in the water; and as soon as the water stops flowing, the algae die and the color fades.

All over the central Plateau, wherever ground water is heated by gases and condensing steam from the underlying igneous intrusives, solution of the silica contained in the rhyolite occurs. As the hot water escapes to the surface, release of pressure and gases allows the precipitation of this silica in a hydrated form. This siliceous deposit is called geyserite or sinter. It is a white or gray mineral, very hard when fresh but rather easily broken up when subjected to the disintegrating action of the elements. It floors the geyser basins to considerable depths. The rims and cones of geysers and hot springs in the siliceous area are built out of geyserite. It is found in a wide variety of depositional forms, varying almost from one geyser to another. The exhibit of thermally deposited minerals shown in the Museum at Old Faithful should be studied, in order to facilitate a moderate appreciation of the artistic splurges Nature has indulged in. The visitor may not notice the extraordinarily beautiful configurations of the geyserite formations unless his attention is called to them. One in particular may often be found where algae has dried up, with the formation of minute towers and needles of geyserite in patterns that would make a cathedral architect green with envy. All factors considered, it must have taken several thousand years to build some of the sinter mounds found in the Park.

Sinter is not totally silica but an amalgamation of materials carried in hot spring water and of life once existing on it. Various minerals and organic material become fused with the silica. So sinter is not completely sterile and can sustain abstemious large plants such as pioneering lodgepole pine. It is a tenuous life. A shift in run-off can flood around the pines and drown them. Such was the fate of the dead trees with white bases that are so common in the Park's geyser basins. Actually upon death the drowned tree begins to petrify. Capillary action lifts mineral-laden water into the base of the trunk. Old cell spaces fill with water. As the water evaporates, it is continually replaced. Thus a cell becomes gradually filled with silica that is left behind by the evaporating water. The woody cell walls remain, but so impregnated with geyserite is the trunk base that it does not rot. Thus, the trees you may be looking at may have been standing for many decades.

No geysers occur in the Park where travertine is the principal deposit. The absence of geysers in these areas has been assumed by many to result from the fact that travertine is much softer than geyserite and unable to withstand the pressure generated at the time of an eruption. This assumption, while true with some of the highly porous travertine, would not hold in the case of more compact specimens such as is found in Terrace Mountain and Liberty Cap. Geysers occur only in areas of boiling springs. The low temperature, and not the deposits, in large measure accounts for the absence of geysers at Mammoth.

RIVERS AND VALLEYS OF YELLOWSTONE

Because of its unusual elevation early Indians referred to the Yellowstone country as the "summit of the world." Despite its being situated in a semi-arid region this high relief has resulted in an annual precipitation much in excess of that of the surrounding country, which is only from eleven to twelve inches. Over the northern section of the plateau the annual precipitation is about eighteen inches. In the southern section, the Snake River watershed, the precipitation is about thirty inches. Thus, from off the mountain and plateaus great rivers descend in every direction. The largest river, Yellowstone, heads near the north base of Younts Peak, about 15 miles southwest of the Park. Its principal tributaries in the Park are the Lamar and Gardner Rivers. The Yellowstone empties into the Missouri in northwestern North Dakota, just east of the Montana line. In the same mountainous area which serves as a heading of the Yellowstone two other important river systems in the west have their origins. The Green River, the principal tributary of the Colorado, and the great southern branch of the Columbia, the Snake River, have their beginnings in and near the Yellowstone country. One of the main branches of the upper Missouri River heads in the geyser basins. The Firehole and Gibbon Rivers unite at Madison Junction to make the Madison. The Madison, Jefferson, and Gallatin Rivers are confluent at Threeforks, Montana, to make the Missouri.

As a result of the Park's general location in the Rocky Mountain system, and the high elevation of its Main Plateau, it is not surprising that the Continental Divide traverses this country. From the Divide's sinuous ridges water flows to different oceans. Two-fifths of the Park drains to the Pacific and three-fifths to the Atlantic via the Gulf of Mexico. One of the interesting features of the serpentine course the Divide pursues through the Park is the great loop which it makes around the watershed of DeLacy Creek.

The road from Old Faithful to West Thumb crosses the loop, hence the Divide, twice in a distance of about 6 miles. The western Divide presents the interesting anomaly of having the waters which drain down the slopes to the west go to the Atlantic, while those which drain to the east go to the Pacific.

According to the U. S. Weather Bureau the mean annual temperature of the main Park Plateau is 39.4° F. This, in addition to the heavily forested landscape, results in drifts and snowfields being over the Park for much the greater portion of the year. The slow melting of winter snow, plus the uneven terrain, has resulted in the formation of numerous lakes and ponds. In the entire Park there are about thirty-six named lakes with a total area of 165 square miles. In addition to these there are scores of unnamed small lakes, many of them kettles and ponds. The four principal lakes are Yellowstone, Shoshone, Heart, and Lewis. All are clustered near the Continental Divide. They differ but little in elevation. Yellowstone Lake is on the Atlantic drainage, the other three on the Pacific.

Yellowstone Lake is the most popular with visitors and is 7,731 feet, nearly a mile and a half above the level of the sea. It has a shoreline of 110 miles and an area of 139 square miles. Its maximum depth is about 300 feet. It is fed almost entirely from the springs and snow drifts of the Absaroka Range. Its waters are cold, clear, and transparent to great depths, but it is subject to heavy southwest winds and at times can be lashed into a tempestuous inland sea. The shape of the lake was compared by the early explorers to the form of the human hand. While the resemblance is exceedingly remote, the westernmost part still carries the designation of "Thumb."

Although mountains are a prime factor in determining the topography of Yellowstone Park, they are, in a practical sense, of less importance than the valleys which lie between them and the streams of which they are the source. As a matter of fact, most of the Park's major attractions are found in its valleys.

The valleys of Yellowstone can be placed into two very broad classifications—open valleys and canyons. The latter are usually more scenic and can be defined as narrow openings between the

On facing page: *Roaring Mountain, where fumeroles discharge steam from several powerful vents near the summit. The heat and the hydrogen sulfide produced by these vents has killed trees on the mountainside over an area about half a mile square.*

Yellowstone National Park Photo.

hills through which the water from the mountains finds its way to the lower country. The best-known one in the Park is the Grand Canyon of the Yellowstone. This canyon extends from below Tower Fall to the Falls of the Yellowstone, a distance of about 25 miles. Its nearly sheer walls rise as much as 1,200 feet above the river and are studded with numerous pinnacles. The upper section of the canyon was eroded and carved in hydrothermally decomposed rhyolite, resulting in many colors of the oxides of iron. Yellow is the dominant color. This brilliant coloration of the canyon walls is responsible for the name "Yellowstone" Park. Were the Park named after its most salient geological feature it would be called Geyser National Park, a name that would be much more readily interpreted by all Park visitors.

There are many other beautiful canyons in the Park. For example, the Gardner River has two: One near the northern entrance to the Park and the other (called Sheepeater Canyon) lies behind Bunsen Peak. On the Firehole there are also two picturesque gorges: One south of Madison Junction and the other in the vicinity of Kepler Cascade, south of the Upper Geyser Basin. Below Virginia Cascade, on the Gibbon River is a small, beautiful canyon that many visitors miss. Of course, as you visit the Park, you may select one of the many other canyons as your favorite.

Of the open valleys of the Park, the combined ones of the Yellowstone and Lamar Rivers, stretching from Crescent Hill and Mount Washburn nearly to the east boundary, are the largest. This open valley area is approximately 25 miles long and 5 to 10 broad. The second largest tract is Hayden Valley, which encompasses the Upper Yellowstone River between the Mud Volcano area and Yellowstone's Grand Canyon. Some of the other open valleys of importance are Elk Park and Gibbon Meadows, on the Gibbon; the Firehole Geyser Basin; Swan Lake Flat and Willow Park, on the Gardner; and the broad area of the Pelican Valley and around Lewis and Shoshone Lakes.

There are upon the various rivers and streams of the Park no fewer than twenty-five interesting waterfalls, where the waters descend from the high-plateau regions to the lower surrounding country. Some of these falls, such as the Lower Falls of the Yellowstone River, 308 feet high—twice the height of famous Niagara Falls—are among the Park's scenic wonders. The Grand Canyon of the Yellowstone, with its beautiful pastel shades and magnificent waterfalls, is worthy of National Park status were there nothing else of interest in the Yellowstone wonderland—*a world apart.*

Chapter 3.

Seeing Yellowstone National Park

Poets have written about Yellowstone, artists have painted it, and even we made a humble attempt to describe it in Chapter 2, but really to believe that such a scenic region is possible, you must see with your own eyes the spouting geysers, bubbling caldrons, giant canyons, and spectacular phenomena, all of which present a flashing brilliance of motion and color which you will never forget. Of all the methods of seeing the Parks—on foot, by automobile, on horseback, or by bus—traveling by motor vehicle is by far the most popular. But it takes time to *see* Yellowstone's many points of interest; thus the wise visitor takes his time finding out why Yellowstone is a world apart.

Most of Yellowstone's points of interest lie on or adjoin the 143-mile-long Grand Loop Road that circumscribes the heart of the Park, leaving few mysteries. Five roads, entering the Park from all sides, lead directly to the "Loop," enabling tours to begin at any desired point. The main roads and major side loops are all paved and maintained for the sight-seer's convenience. But motor vehicles should not be operated outside constructed roadways or designated parking areas. Also remember that the Park's roads have numerous curves and grades. Excessive speed may spell major tragedy. *Courtesy* and *caution* must be exercised to avoid accidents. (The speed limit is 45 miles per hour except where posted otherwise.)

Starting with Mammoth Hot Springs, the major points of interest are listed and described here in the order in which you will find them in going counterclockwise around the Grand Loop.

MAMMOTH HOT SPRINGS

The administrative and business headquarters of the Park are located at Mammoth Hot Springs. Here, graceful terraces rise in great stair-like tiers. They are formed by travertine deposits, which are colored by living algae, that continue to build and form new basins. The mineral waters fill these basins, then cascade with reflected color to the ground.

Gateway to Mammoth may be made by way of the Northern Entrance road (*5.3 miles in length*) and through the *Roosevelt Arch,* which was dedicated by President Theodore Roosevelt in 1903. The two prominent peaks on the west as you enter the Park are *Electric Peak* and *Sepulcher Mountain.* (The feature which gave the latter its name is very apparent from this point.) Soon after passing under the archway the road enters the *Gardner Canyon,* which it follows for about 4 miles. The cliffs on the east side which are bold and precipitous, plus the foaming *Gardner River,* are the major beauty features of the Canyon. At *Eagles' Nest Rock* (a misnomer), the nest of an osprey can usually be seen on the summit of the pinnacle. About 2 miles further along you come to *Hot River,* an immense stream of hot water which comes from an opening in the rocks, and discharges directly into the Gardner River. The winding entrance road, which rises better than 600 feet in the distance of a little more than a mile, carries you from the valley of the Gardner to Mammoth and its famous hot springs.

(*Note:* Cumulative mileages are used in the tables in this chapter; however, speedometer mileages will tend to vary between individual automobiles. For further information on trail head numbers, see Chapter 5, while campground data is given in Chapter 10.)

Miles	*Points of Interest*	*Miles*
0.0	Roosevelt Arch, North Entrance to Park	5.3
0.5	*Junction.* Service road. Also Entrance and Ranger Stations	4.8
0.9	Trail Head 7—Rescue Creek Trail	4.4
1.6	Eagles' Nest Rock viewpoint	3.7
1.7	Gardner River crossing	3.6
3.0	Gardner River crossing	2.3
3.1	Montana-Wyoming boundary line	2.2
3.6	Hot River viewpoint	1.7
4.4	Mammoth campground	0.9
5.3	Mammoth Junction	0.0

On facing page: *Norris Geyser Basin. The thermal features of the area make this one of the most exciting sections of Yellowstone. It is often referred to by visitors as Dante's Inferno. Seventeen major geysers are in the Basin, and wooden walks, as shown, let visitors observe the thermal display close at hand.* **Union Pacific Railroad Photo.**

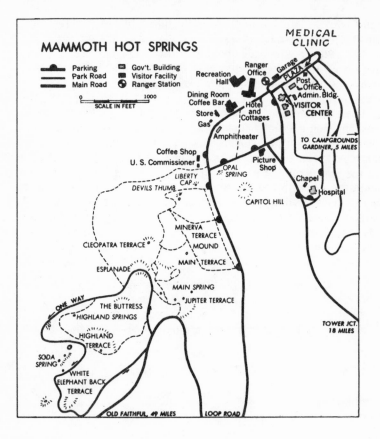

MAMMOTH HOT SPRINGS

Parking
Park Road
Main Road

Gov't. Building
Visitor Facility
Ranger Station

0   1000
SCALE IN FEET

MEDICAL CLINIC

Ranger Office
Garage
PLAZA
Post Office
Admin. Bldg.
VISITOR CENTER

Recreation Hall

Dining Room
Coffee Bar
Store
Gas

Hotel and Cottages

Amphitheater

TO CAMPGROUNDS
GARDINER, 5 MILES

Coffee Shop
U. S. Commissioner

Picture Shop

OPAL SPRING

LIBERTY CAP
DEVILS THUMB

Chapel

Hospital

CAPITOL HILL

MINERVA TERRACE
MOUND

CLEOPATRA TERRACE

MAIN TERRACE

ESPLANADE

MAIN SPRING
JUPITER TERRACE

ONE WAY
THE BUTTRESS
HIGHLAND SPRINGS

TOWER JCT.
18 MILES

HIGHLAND TERRACE

SODA SPRING

WHITE ELEPHANT BACK TERRACE

OLD FAITHFUL, 49 MILES   LOOP ROAD

Mammoth is the only point in the Park where an extensive modification of natural conditions has been permitted. Many of the Park buildings were part of old Fort Yellowstone. As previously stated, the Park was patrolled by soldiers until 1916, and Mammoth was Fort Yellowstone which played an important part in the history of the early northwest. The buildings were the homes of the commissioned and non-commissioned officers of the old fort. They are now occupied by the Park officials; the superintendent, assistant superintendent, chief electrician, chief engineer, a ranger station, museum, visitor center, etc. The large open space between the terraces and the buildings was the parade ground of the old fort.

Among the natural features of interest accessible from this

locality are the *Hot Springs Terraces*. The formation about these springs, it will be remembered, is calcareous, and to this fact is due its distinctive character, so different from the silica formations that prevail nearly everywhere else in the Park. The most visited active springs include *Orange Spring, Jupiter, Pulpit, Opal, Minerva, Narrow Gauge* and the *White Elephant Terraces*. *Liberty Cap* is an extinct spring cone 37 feet high, formed by travertine deposit from hot water which flowed from an orifice at its top.

Ranging over the terrace's formation are hot-spring caves, steam-vents, peculiar deposits, and curiosities without number to hold the interest of everyone. Among them are *Devil's Kitchen, Cheops Mound, Bath Lake, Poison Caves,* and *Stygian Cave.* In many of the caves there is an accumulation of carbon dioxide gas in sufficient quantities to destroy animal life, especially birds. Actually, Stygian Cave at the extreme upper end of the active terraces, is the most notorious in this respect.

Guided terrace and nature walks, given by Park naturalists, are scheduled at various times during the day. These are supplemented by the Mammoth Terrace Nature trail and the Clematis Gulch self-guiding trail. While at the visitor center, be sure to take a stroll through the museum which features exhibits on the wildlife, geology, and human history of the Yellowstone country. Evening campfire talks are presented in the Mammoth Amphitheater from mid-June through mid-September.

Mammoth Hot Springs to Norris Junction (20.6 miles)

When taking the Grand Loop south from Mammoth, and after passing the terraces, the road climbs past the *Hoodoos.* A short one-way loop road gives you an opportunity to study these interesting rock formations of travertine. The lines of stratification show how these enormous rocks have been tipped from their original horizontal position, but the disturbing cause has affected no two alike.

Back again on the Grand Loop, you will find that it leads into *Golden Gate Canyon,* through which the *Glen Creek* finds its way between *Terrace Mountain* and *Bunsen Peak*. This canyon is considered one of the star features of the Park's scenery and receives its name because of the yellow lichens (see page 130) that cover the cliff rock here. The present *Golden Gate bridge,* or viaduct of cantilever construction, on which you are traveling, was completed by the National Park Service in 1934. The 1959 earthquake in Yellowstone caused a rockslide at Golden Gate that did considerable damage. There is an earthquake exhibit at the head of the Canyon. Also at the head of the Canyon is *Rustic Falls,* a small (47 feet high) but interesting waterfall of Glen Creek.

Leaving Golden Gate Canyon through *Kingman Pass,* you next come to a junction with *Bunsen Peak loop road.* This 7-mile one-way, winding road, with several rather steep grades, takes you past some of the most interesting scenery in the Park, and rejoins the main highway back at Mammoth Hot Springs terraces. (Trailers should *not* attempt this road.) After a short ride across the open country of *Swan Lake Flat,* this side road permits you to view the 800-foot deep *Sheepeater Canyon* of the Gardner River and the *Osprey Falls* at its head. (The canyon was named after the Sheep-eater tribe of Indians.) Many people consider that this canyon ranks next to the Grand Canyon of the Yellowstone as the most impressive in the Park. Osprey Falls is also one of the largest cataracts in the Park and an interesting trail leads to its foot. Across the gorge are the *Sheepeater Cliffs.* After leaving Sheep-eater Canyon, the road affords a panoramic view of the Gardner River valley and the great mountains and terraces surrounding Mammoth Hot Springs.

Picking up your journey southward toward Norris Junction on the Loop Road, you will pass several small lakes—*Swan Lake, Beaver Lake, Twin Lakes,* and *Nymph Lake;* a few streams—*Gardner River, Obsidian Creek,* and *Lemonade Creek;* and some famous springs—*Apollinaris Spring* (mineral water), *Crystal Spring* (cold), and *Clearwater, Bijah,* and *Roadside Springs* (hot). You may even wish to stop at Jim Bridger's mountain of glass (see page 3). This is the *Obsidian Cliff,* which is com-posed of a type of volcanic glass, black as coal. The Indians once quarried implements of hunt and war here. When the first road was built in this region, under the direction of Colonel P. W. Norris, a novel method was used to clear away the rock of the Obsidian Cliff. This glassy material was broken into fragments by heating it with fires and then dashing cold water upon it.

After passing Obsidian Cliff, there is an increase in thermal activities. *Roaring Mountain* is a high hill near the road, with powerful steam vents. The heat and the hydrogen sulfide produced by these vents killed the trees on the mountainside over the space of half a square mile. Between the road and the base of the moun-tain is a body of yellow-green water called *Lemonade Lake.* The *Frying Pan Spring,* reached further along the loop road, is a small basin of geyserite, on the right of the road, vigorously stewing away in a manner which reminds one of a kitchen skillet in oper-ation.

44

Miles	Points of Interest	Miles
0.0	Mammoth Junction	20.6
0.3	*Junction.* North to center of Mammoth Village and road to Tower Junction (see page 68)	20.3
0.4	Liberty Cap parking area	20.2
0.5	Minerva Terrace parking area	20.1
0.8	Main Terrace parking area	19.8
1.3	*Junction.* Bunsen Peak loop road (One-way—do *not* enter)	19.3
1.8	Trail to Jupiter Terrace	18.8
2.1	*Junction.* Terrace loop road (1.7 miles)	18.5
3.8	*Junction.* Hoodoo loop road (0.5 mile)	16.8
4.6	Golden Gate Canyon parking area	16.0
4.8	Rustic Falls viewpoint	15.8
4.9	*Junction.* Bunsen Peak loop road (7.0 miles)	15.7
5.8	Swan Lake viewpoint	12.8
8.2	Gardner River crossing	12.4
8.5	*Junction.* Indian Creek campground road	12.1
10.1	Willow Park parking area	10.5
10.7	Moose Exhibit parking area	9.9
11.2	Apollinaris Spring. Near by (on west side of road) is Trail Head 13—Mount Holmes trail.	9.4
12.0	Crystal Spring	8.6
12.6	Obsidian Cliff Exhibit and parking area	8.0
13.0	Beaver Lake	7.6
13.7	Public *emergency* roadside telephone	6.9
13.9	Lemonade Creek crossing	6.7
15.6	Clearwater Springs	5.0
15.8	Semi-Centennial Geyser (formerly the most northerly geyser; now just a larger hot spring pool)	4.8
16.2	Roaring Mountain parking area	4.4
16.5	Twin Lakes	4.1
17.7	Bijah Spring	2.9
18.3	Roadside Spring	2.3
18.5	Frying Pan Springs	2.1
20.4	*Junction.* Road to Norris campground. Norris Ranger Station	0.2
20.6	*Norris Junction.* Norris-Canyon cutoff-road	0.0

The Norris-Canyon cutoff-road is a fine highway (12.1 miles) that leads from *Norris Junction* to *Canyon Junction.* Along this road at a point about 3 miles from Norris Junction there is a one-way (eastbound) loop to *Virginia Cascade,* a picturesque waterfall in a rocky canyon of considerable beauty. This cascade is not a cataract, but a rocky slide on which the water glides down some 60 feet over the slippery surface of the rock. Trail Head 14 (trail to *Cygnet Lakes*) and Trail Head 15 (trail to *Grebe Lake*) are also off the Norris-Canyon cutoff-road.

45

Norris Junction to Madison Junction (13.7 miles)

Continuing south on the Grand Loop Road, your next major point of interest is the Norris Visitor Center, in the heart of *Norris Geyser Basin.* To many people this is the most exciting geyser basin in the Park. Some of its thermal features are set within a great hollowed-out bowl called the *Porcelain Basin,* within which roaring steam vents provide eerie sound effects as you walk through. Geysers and bubbling springs add to the activity. Here, as in no other part of the Park, the visitor is brought face-to-face with the forces that have made Yellowstone what it is. Comments invariably reflect that emotion, whether they be an allusion to Dante's *Inferno,* or a "sage-brusher" comment, "This sure is the lid on Hades and it ain't clamped down very tight, either."

The Porcelain Basin walk—on your own or naturalist-conducted (hourly from mid-June through early-September)—is about a half-mile loop and takes you past most of its varied thermal features. For those who like a longer hike, the *Black Basin* self-guiding trail will take you over the entire southern basin in less than 2 miles of walking. While taking these trips, as in any of the Park's geyser basins, be sure to stay on the constructed wooden walks; in many places the earth's crust is extremely thin and walking on it is dangerous. Take care not to slip or step into hot pools. Children must be closely attended; leave your pets in your car. Before leaving the area, be sure to see the Visitor Center and Museum, with its unusual dioramas of the geology of thermal areas.

NORRIS GEYSER BASIN

Name	Height in feet	Duration	Interval
Arsenic Geyser	6-10	15-20 minutes	Irregular
Basin Geyser	20-40	Variable	2-4 minutes
Big Alcove Geyser	6-10	Rather constant	None
Blue Geyser	12-15	Variable	Days
Constant Geyser	30-40	5-10 seconds	Several an hour
Dark Cavern Geyser	10-20	Variable	Several an hour
Echinus Geyser	40-70	3-5 minutes	1-2 hours
Feisty Geyser	6-10	Variable	Several a day
Fireball Geyser	4-8	Variable	Several an hour
Ledge Geyser	75-125	1-5 hours	Days
Little Whirligig Geyser	10-15	Almost constant	2-5 seconds
Minute Geyser	3-12	30-40 minutes	10-24 hours
Perpetual Spouter	3-5	Constant	None
Pinwheel Geyser	10-15	1-3 minutes	15-25 minutes
Steamboat Geyser	2-3	2-3 minutes	3-4 minutes
(see page 28)	300-350	Variable	7-14 days
Valentine Geyser	50-70	1-3 hours	Irregular
Vixen Geyser	15-25	1-5 minutes	Irregular

The Loop Road passes through the midst of the Norris Geyser Basin, in close proximity to some of the boiling springs and geysers, and does not get clear of the hot ground until it enters *Elk Park,* a meadow area. Then the road follows the *Gibbon River* to within 4 miles of its mouth and continues through *Gibbon Geyser Basin* —a small group of hot springs, geysers, and other thermal features that begins at the northern edge of *Gibbon Meadows* and continues southward into the *Gibbon Canyon* as far as the Beryl Spring region. The most interesting phenomena include the *Gibbon Hill Geyser, Chocolate Pots, Artists Paintpots, Monument Geyser, and Beryl Spring.* The Monument Geyser Basin and Artist Paintpot trails are two short walks that you should take while in the Gibbon area. Further along the *Gibbon Canyon,* you will come to *Gibbon Falls,* a beautiful waterfall that is worth photographing.

Following the road southward, you will come to *Madison Junction.* The Visitor Center here tells the story of the founding of the park in its exhibits and in the views from its picture window, which looks out on the very campsite at the junction of the *Gibbon* and *Firehole Rivers* where the Yellowstone National Park idea was first effectively expressed (see page 5). Speaking of camping, there is a large campground at Madison Junction, and campfire talks are given at its amphitheater (mid-June-early September).

Miles	*Points of Interest*	*Miles*
0.0	Norris Junction	13.7
0.6	Norris Visitor Center and	
	Norris Geyser Basin parking area	13.1
0.9	Minute Geyser	12.8
1.4	Ferric and Cupric Caldron (small, colorful hot springs)	12.3
1.7	Elk Park	12.0
3.1	Chocolate Pots (hot springs)	10.6
3.5	Gibbon Meadows	10.2
4.3	Artists Paintpots parking area and trail	9.4
5.1	Monument Geyser parking area and trail	8.6
5.4	Beryl Springs parking area	8.3
6.2	Gibbon River crossing	7.5
6.7	Public *emergency* roadside telephone	7.0
7.2	Gibbon River crossing	6.5
8.4	Iron Spring (cold mineral-water spring)	5.3
8.9	Gibbon Falls parking area	4.8
9.7	*Junction.* Mesa service road—rejoins Grand Loop Road below Madison Junction (8.2 miles)	4.0
13.1	Terrace Spring (hot-water pond)	0.6
13.7	Madison Junction. Madison Visitor Center and campground.	
	West Entrance road.	0.0

The *Western Entrance* is 13.9 miles west of Madison Junction. From *West Yellowstone entrance station,* the highway traverses a beautifully wooded flat called *Christmas Tree Park* beyond which the Madison River valley narrows until its walls are rather precipitous. The highway winds through this interesting canyon and ends where *Firehole* and *Gibbon Rivers* join to form the *Madison.* Trail Head 12 (*Gneiss Creek trail* and *Old Fountain trail*) leaves from the Western Entrance road, about 9½ miles from Madison Junction.

Madison Junction to Old Faithful (16.2 miles)

From Madison Junction southward, the Grand Loop Road follows the valley of the *Firehole River* to *Nez Percé Creek.* This creek is the major tributary of the Firehole, and is of historic interest from the fact that the route of Chief Joseph in 1877 was along its valley. But, before reaching the Creek, there is an interesting side road through *Firehole Canyon,* and past *Firehole Falls* and the *Cascades of the Firehole River.* This one-way, southbound road is about 2 miles and rejoins the Grand Loop Road.

After crossing over Nez Percé Creek, you reach the first of three thermal areas of the Firehole—the Lower Geyser Basin. Actually, it is the largest thermal area in the Park, and groups of hot springs are widely scattered over the entire basin. However, with two exceptions, the principal ones are found on the east side. Numerous mud springs are found near the west side and can be seen by taking self-guided, half-mile *Fountain Paint Pot* Nature Trail. This trail also takes you by *Silex Spring, Red Spouter, Leather Pool, Spasm Geyser, Morning Geyser, Clepsydra Geyser, Celestine Pool,* and *Jelly Geyser.* Nearby, too, is *Gentian Pool,* the color of Yellowstone's official flower, the Rocky Mountain fringed gentian.

Off the Loop Road in Lower Geyser Basin, a 3-mile loop road takes you past *Firehole Lake* (Pool), one of the largest hot lakes in the Park. (The lake itself is reached by a one-third mile foot trail.) This takes you past such worthy geysers as *Great Fountain* and *White Dome;* pools like *Surprise* and *Hot Lake;* and springs like *Broken Egg* and *Black Warrior.* The height, duration and interval of the major geysers in the Lower Geyser Basin appear in the table on the following page.

Next major stop on the Grand Loop is *Midway Geyser Basin.* This basin is topographically a part of the Lower Basin. It was no doubt given basin status because dense forests to the north and west separate it from other hot-spring groups in the Lower Basin. Midway's hot springs extend along the Firehole River for a distance of about a mile, and then for an additional mile along the *Rabbit Creek* drainage. Springs are numerous (the *Grand Pris-*

LOWER GEYSER BASIN

Name	Height in feet	Duration	Interval
Bead Geyser	10-12	1-1½ minutes	20-3 minutes
Bellefontaine Geyser	6-8	2-3 minutes	Infrequent
Clepsydra Geyser	20-40	3-6 hours	Infrequent
Great Fountain	75-200	35-60 minutes	5-17 hours
Jelly Geyser	1-15	31 minutes	9-30 minutes
Jet Geyser	10-12	20-30 seconds	5-60 minutes*
Kaleidoscope	25-30	2 minutes	3-45 minutes*
Mask Geyser	6-10	3-4 minutes	3-4 hours
Morning Geyser	20-250	45-60 minutes	2-3 weekly*
Mud Spring	3-15	10-15 minutes	6-8 hours
Pink Cone	12-18	1-2 hours	8-10 hours
Red Spouter	6-8	Months	Months
Silex Spring	1-3	2-3 minutes	1-4 hours*
Snort Geyser	15-20	Days	Days
Spasm Geyser	3-35	10-15 minutes	Irregular
Steady Geyser	6-15	Constant	None
Sub Geyser	3-6	1 minute	3-5 minutes*
Thud Geyser	12-15	3-4 minutes	3-4 hours*
White Dome Geyser	18-30	1½-2½ minutes	15-90 minutes

* Sometimes inactive for long periods.

matic Spring is the largest spring in Yellowstone) along both drainages, but geysers are relatively scarce. Only ten springs are known to be geysers; with the exception of *Excelsior,* all are small. Excelsior Geyser was once the most powerful in the Park. Excelsior last played in 1888, when it shot 300 feet into the air; it still gives forth some 1½ billion gallons of scalding water annually. The steam from its crater fills the whole basin at sunset when the air is cool. All the points of interest in this geyser basin can be seen from a short foot trail.

Continuing southward along the Loop Road, it finally leads into the *Upper Geyser Basin* region. The area of the basin is about 2 square miles, being about 2 miles long, expanding to an average width of about a mile. It narrows on both ends. *Biscuit Basin* marks the lower extremity of the basin, while *Old Faithful* stands at the head. It is surrounded by rocky cliffs, which stand out prominently on the west, northwest, and east. *Biscuit Basin,* about 2¼ miles from Old Faithful, and *Black Sand Basin,* one mile from Old Faithful, are separate divisions within the Upper Basin. The valley is not only drained by the Firehole River, but by *Iron Creek* and the *Little Firehole River* which enter the main stream in the Biscuit Basin area. The important geysers are located near the

main river, most of them within a distance of about one mile of each other.

The Biscuit Basin group of hot springs was so named because of the biscuit-shaped geyserite deposits around *Sapphire Pool.* These, however, were mainly destroyed when this geyser broke loose and became violent during the earthquake of 1959. Its tumultuous waters tore up and washed away large chunks of its crust. In addition to Sapphire Pool, you will find the *Black Opal Pool, Wall Pool, Mustard Spring, Jewel Geyser, Shell Spring, Black Pearl* and *Avoca Spring* along the basin's almost half-mile walk.

On the way toward the main portion of the Upper Geyser Basin, you pass the *Morning Glory Pool.* Its exquisite bordering and the deep cerulean hue (caused by a yellow algae) of its transparent waters make it an object of ceaseless admiration. But many appreciative persons feel that the beauty of this pool has been marred by *thoughtless* people throwing away their money into it.

Mortar and *Fan Geysers* are close by the Firehole on the east bank, not far above the Morning Glory. The *Riverside* is also on the east bank at a point near where the road crosses the river. It is rather an inconspicuous object when not in eruption, and one would scarcely suspect it of being one of the more powerful geysers in the Park. It spouts obliquely across the river and not, like most geysers, vertically.

Between the road and the west bank of Firehole, there are such fine geysers as *Spa, Rocket, Bijou, Mastiff, Grotto, Surprise,* and *Giant.* The latter has thrown water over 200 feet in the air and discharged as much as one million gallons in an eruption. Unfortunately, this magnificent geyser is inactive and asleep for long periods of time.

Near the Grotto Geyser, a 2-mile scenic road leaves the Grand Loop and goes past the *Black Sand Basin.* Along the way you pass such thermal features as *Daisy, Comet, Splendid, Spouter, Whistle,* and *Cliff Geysers; Brilliant, Bonita Sunset, Rainbow, Algal, Emerald, Black Sand,* and *Handkerchief Pools;* and *Punch Bowl, Green,* and *Three Sisters Springs.* A short walk takes you to most of the features that cannot be seen from your automobile. By the way, the black sand in the basin is finely fragmented volcanic rock.

The Black Sand Basin road rejoins the Grand Loop just before reaching *Old Faithful Inn,* the world's largest log hostelry. This unique and rustic structure has been host to presidents and royalty since 1904. A little further along, you reach Old Faithful Village.

On facing page: *Riverside Geyser erupts over the Firehole River.*
Union Pacific Railroad Photo.

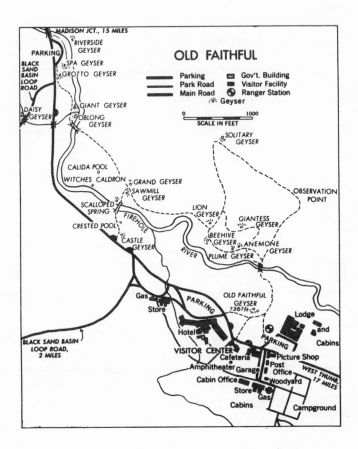

This bustling area's activities are timed to the performances of the world's most renowned geyser, which was fully described on page 29. Each evening during the summer, the first eruption of Old Faithful Geyser after 9 p.m. is illuminated.

In addition to Old Faithful we find such spectacular geysers as the *Lion, Lioness, Vault, Little Squirt, Plume, Sawmill, Beehive, Surge, Pump, Castle, Giantess,* and *Grand.* To many people, Grand is the most spectacular geyser in the Park. The huge column of water that is suddenly blasted into the air does not play with a steady forceful stream as does Old Faithful, but has a rocketing or jet-like type of function. The main column is made up of many

52

separate, rocketing jets of water. This display usually lasts about two minutes, at times longer. The water column then drops rather abruptly, with the water about and in the bowl rushing back into the momentarily empty vent. Before the spectator catches his breath from the first imposing display, the water again rises in the crater as before and again blasts into the air. After a moment of action of even greater magnitude than the previous display, the column again suddenly drops, repeating the previous performance. During an eruption of the Grand, which usually lasts for about twenty minutes, there are as a general rule about eleven or twelve separate eruptions of the character described. Eight are the fewest observed and forty-four the most.

There are many interesting hot pools along the Upper Geyser Basin walks, including *Chinaman's Spring*. This spring was supposed to have been used by a clever Oriental in the old days when he did the washing for a big hotel. He set his tent over the spring and thus had an unlimited supply of hot water. One day, so the story goes, the spring erupted, the tent went up never to come down again and the Chinaman was picked up by a missionary on the streets of Shanghai three months later.

The height, duration, and interval of the major geysers in the Upper Basin appear in the accompanying table:

Name	Height in feet	Duration	Interval
Anemone Geyser	5-6	Minutes to hours	Frequent
Artemisia Geyser	15-35	13-15 minutes	24-30 hours
Atomizer Geyser	20-40	1-10 minutes	Daily
Avoca Spring	3-12	Seconds	1-1½ minutes
Beehive Geyser	100-150	5-8 minutes	2-5 days*
Bijou Geyser	4-20	Almost constant	None
Biscuit Basin Geyser	70-80	4-5 minutes	Infrequent
Black Pearl Geyser	4-8	Seconds	Frequent
Cascade Geyser	15-20	2-3 minutes	1-2 hours*
Castle Geyser	30-80	15-60 minutes	4-10 hours
Catfish Geyser	10-35	2-20 minutes	Frequent*
Cliff Geyser	20-40	2-3 hours	6-15 hours*
Comet Geyser	4-6	1 minute	4 minutes
Coral Geyser	6-10	5-8 minutes	8-15 minutes
Daisy Geyser	65-75	2-4 minutes	1½-3 hours*
Fan Geyser	100-125	10-15 minutes	Infrequent
Giant Geyser	180-225	1-1½ hours	2-14 days*
Giantess Geyser	75-200	12-36 hours	Infrequent
Grand Geyser	160-180	15 minutes-1½ hours	8 hours to days

(*Continued on next page.*)

Name	Height in feet	Duration	Interval
Grotto Geyser	8-40	1-2 hours	1-12 hours
Jewel Geyser	12-24	1-1½ minutes	5-8 minutes
Link Geyser	4-75	12-15 minutes	3-4 hours*
Lion Geyser	50-60	4-5 minutes	1-2 hours*
Lioness Geyser	20-40	5-10 minutes	Infrequent
Little Brother Geyser	15-25	4-6 minutes	15-20 minutes*
Little Cub Geyser	10-15	15-20 minutes	1-4 hours
Little Squirt	3-6	Days	Days
Mastiff Geyser	4-100	Variable	Infrequent
Mortar Geyser	30-60	10-15 minutes	Infrequent
Mustard Spring	2-4	1-2 minutes	5-8 minutes
Oblong Geyser	20-40	6-9 minutes	2-10 hours
Old Faithful Geyser	100-185	2-5 minutes	35-95 minutes
Plume Geyser	25-35	1-4 minutes	23-30 minutes*
Riverside Geyser	75-80	15-20 minutes	5½-9 hours
Rocket Geyser	6-40	3-5 minutes	1-12 hours
Sapphire Pool	10-75	2-8 minutes	10-30 minutes
Sawmill Geyser	15-35	1-3 hours	1-3 hours*
Solitary Geyser	20-25	2 minutes	2-6 minutes
Spa Geyser	35-40	1-2 minutes	Infrequent
Spanker Geyser	4-6	Constant	Constant
Spasmodic Geyser	3-20	20-40 minutes	Daily
Splendid Geyser	100-165	2-10 minutes	Hours to days*
Spouter Geyser	3-7	15-20 hours	Frequent
Sunset Lake	3-8	1 minute	Frequent
Surge Geyser	5-6	Seconds	4-6 minutes
Surprise Geyser	30-65	17-60 minutes	6-12 hours*
Tardy Geyser	6-10	1 to several hours	1 to several hours
Three Sisters (North Vent)	3-4	1 minute	4-6 minutes
Three Sisters (East Vent)	15-20	3 minutes	35-50 minutes*
Turban Geyser	5-10	3-60 minutes	15-25 minutes
Turtle Geyser	15-25	4-10 minutes	Infrequent
Whistle Geyser	30-40	2-3 hours	Infrequent
Vault Geyser	10-15	4-5 minutes	50-60 minutes*
Vent Geyser	20-30	15-60 minutes	8 hours to days

* Sometimes inactive for long periods.

While in the Upper Basin area, do not miss the *Geyser Hill* and *Gentian* self-guiding nature trails east of the Old Faithful. For photographs, walk from Old Faithful to Observation Point. The climax of this walk is a view of the Upper Basin (with Old Faithful just opposite) from a height of some 300 feet. Also be sure to stop at Old Faithful Visitor Center, open daily May 1 through

November 1, to see the exhibits that explain the hot spring and geyser activity of the surrounding area. Probable eruption times of the major geysers are posted here daily. Evening campfire talks are presented each evening in the Old Faithful Amphitheater from May 15 to mid-October.

Miles	Points of Interest	Miles
0.0	Madison Junction	16.2
0.5	*Junction.* Firehole Canyon road	15.7
2.2	*Junction.* Mesa road	14.0
2.3	*Junction.* Firehole Canyon road	
	(One-way—do *not* enter)	13.9
5.6	Public *emergency* roadside telephone	10.6
5.7	*Junction.* Fountain Freight road—	
	service road to Upper	
	Geyser Basin (7.6 miles)	10.5
6.2	Nez Percé Creek crossing	10.0
6.5	*Junction.* Mary Mountain truck road—Trail Head 25	
	(Mary Mountain trail) starts about 1 mile up this road	9.7
8.1	Lower Geyser Basin. Fountain Paint	
	Pots parking area on west side.	
	Junction—Firehole Lake loop	
	road on east side (2.7 miles)	8.1
9.1	*Junction.* Firehole Lake loop road	7.1
10.2	Midway Geyser Basin parking area	6.0
11.4	Rabbit Creek crossing	4.8
11.5	*Junction.* Fountain Freight road	4.7
13.9	Biscuit Basin parking area	2.3
14.6	Morning Glory Pool	1.6
14.7	Firehole River crossing	1.5
14.8	Riverside Geyser parking area	1.4
15.0	*Junction.* Black Sand Basin loop road (2.1 miles)	1.2
15.6	Castle Geyser parking area	0.6
15.8	*Junction.* Black Sand Basin loop road	0.4
16.0	Old Faithful Inn	0.2
16.2	Old Faithful Visitor Center	0.0

Old Faithful to West Thumb Junction (16.9 miles)

From Old Faithful, the Grand Loop Road ascends the valley of the Firehole River to the mouth of *Spring Creek,* which stream it follows to the Continental Divide. For 7 miles it then lies on the Pacific slope, after which it descends the mountains to the Yellowstone Lake, which is on the Atlantic slope. The first point of interest that you come to is the *Kepler Cascade of the Firehole*—a series of falls 90 to 150 feet in height, between perpendicular canyon walls. A short distance beyond, a side road follows the Firehole River up to the *Lone Star Geyser*. This geyser is important chiefly because of its fine cone. It plays frequently to a height of 25 to 35 feet.

The first crossing of the Continental Divide, at elevation of 8,261 feet, is through a narrow, rocky gorge called *Craig Pass*. *Isa Lake,* athwart the Continental Divide at Craig Pass, empties into both the Atlantic and Pacific Oceans. The golden water lilies, which cover its surface from early summer until frost, are used as food by many small animals.

The next spot you will wish to stop is at *Shoshone Point*. It overlooks *Shoshone Lake* and the broad basin surrounding it, and gives an excellent view of the Grand Tetons. The lake, itself, has an area of about 12 square miles and a most picturesque shoreline. On its west shore is a large geyser basin which includes several most interesting thermal features. Shoshone Lake can only be reached by trail (see Chapter 5) and by boat (see Chapter 8). But, in the *Shoshone Geyser Basin,* there are no railings or board walks to discipline your strolling, so be extra careful; the ground is thin, the water is hot, and you are a long way from help.

From Shoshone Point, the road again ascends to the Continental Divide (elevation 8,364 feet), and then drops down the Atlantic slope towards the Yellowstone Valley. At *Lake View,* you see the whole vista of *Yellowstone Lake* spreading out before you. Far to the left and right, along the distant eastern shore extends the Absaroka Range of mountains. Continuing downward from Lake View, the road passes, a little further on, *Duck Lake,* a fine, small pond of genuine beauty. A short drive now brings you to *West Thumb Junction.*

Miles	*Points of Interest*	*Miles*
0.0	Old Faithful Visitor Center	16.9
0.7	Trail Head 24—trail to Mallard Lake	16.2
1.6	Kepler Cascades of the Firehole	15.3
1.7	Junction. Road to Lone Star Geyser (2.6 miles)	15.2
4.2	Spring Creek crossing. Public *emergency* roadside telephone	12.7
6.8	Isa Lake and the Continental Divide (8,261 feet)	10.1
7.9	DeLacy Creek crossing. Trail Head 23— trail to Shoshone Lake	9.0
8.4	Shoshone Point (Shoshone region viewpoint)	8.5
12.6	Continental Divide (8,364 feet)	4.3
15.9	Lake View (Yellowstone Lake viewpoint)	1.0
16.4	Duck Lake	0.5
16.9	West Thumb Junction. South Entrance from Grand Teton National Park	0.0

56

Lone Star Geyser, Yellowstone National Park.

The major objects of interest on the southern approach road from Grand Teton National Park to the Grand Loop, are *Moose Falls* on *Crawfish Creek, Lewis Canyon,* the *Falls of the Lewis River,* and *Lewis Lake.* From this road, a trail leaves for *Heart Lake,* one of the prettiest in the Park. Near it, on a tributary of the *Witch Creek,* is a small but interesting geyser basin. The principal features are the *Deluge, Spike,* and *Rustic Geysers,* and the *Fissure Group of Springs.* Remember that there are no board walks or protection here; so be careful.

Miles	*Points of Interest*	*Miles*
0.0	South Entrance Ranger Station.	
	Trail Head 20—Snake River Lookout trail.	22.0
0.3	Snake River campground	21.7
1.5	Moose Falls viewpoint	20.5
7.9	Lewis Canyon parking area	14.1
10.3	The Falls of the Lewis River	11.7
13.7	*Junction.* Road to Lewis Lake	
	campground. Boat launching ramp here.	8.3
14.0	Lewis Lake viewpoint	8.0
14.3	Trail Head 21—Heart Lake trail	7.7
17.9	Continental Divide crossing (7,988 feet).	
	Trail Head 22—Riddle Lake trail.	4.1
20.4	*Junction.* Grant Village road	
	to campground and visitor's	
	area. Boat launching ramp. The ten-mile	
	Flat Mountain foot trail leaves from here	
	to Delusion Lake.	1.6
22.0	West Thumb Junction	0.0

West Thumb Junction to Lake Junction (22.9 miles)

At West Thumb, there is an important center of thermal activity. The principal features are the *Paint Pots;* two of the largest and most beautiful hot springs—*Abyss* and *Black Pools*—in the Park; a couple of small geysers; and the celebrated *Fishing Cone,* a hot-spring mound surrounded by cold lake waters. Brief geyser walks are conducted by a Park naturalist on daylong duty in the area, plus a conducted, two-hour hike to scenic overlook of Yellowstone Lake; there is a self-guiding geyser walk and an evening campfire program.

There are comparatively few attractions on the road from West Thumb to *Lake Junction.* However, several excellent points give

Aerial view of West Thumb thermal area.

a fine view of Yellowstone Lake and the surrounding mountains. About 19 miles from West Thumb a short side road takes you to the *Natural Bridge,* an arch of stone about 40 feet in height and 30 feet in span.

A short distance further on the Grand Loop Road, you pass two-hundred-boat *Bridge Bay marina* and *campgrounds,* and then the *Lake Hotel* and *Lake Lodge.* Finally, you join the *East Entrance Road* at *Lake Junction.*

West Thumb Junction to Lake Junction (22.9 miles)

Miles	Points of Interest	Miles
0.0	West Thumb Junction	22.9
3.0	Buff Point	19.9
5.4	Arnica Creek crossing	17.5
9.0	Mount Sheridan viewpoint	13.9
11.1	Pumice Point viewpoint	11.8
17.6	Gull Point viewpoint	5.3
18.9	*Junction.* Natural Bride road (1.2 miles)	4.0
19.1	*Junction.* Bridge Bay road marina and campground (0.4 miles). Boat launching ramp.	3.8
21.2	Lake Hospital	1.7
21.3	Lake Hotel	1.6
21.9	Lake Lodge	1.0
22.9	Lake Junction. Road to East Entrance Station (26.3 miles)	0.0

From the East Entrance Station, the road starts a climb of more than 1,500 feet to the summit of *Sylvan Pass* in the Absaroka Range. This pass is flanked by lofty mountains—*Avalanche Peak* and *Mount Hoyt* on the north, and *Grizzly* and *Top Notch Peaks* on the south. At the very summit of Sylvan Pass a waterfall comes tumbling down from the cliffs on the south, and flows into a small pond named *Lake Eleanor.*

On the other (west) side pass, *Sylvan Lake,* near the source of *Clear Creek,* is another of the Park's beauties. It is not a large body of water, but its irregular shoreline makes up a picture which appeals to the artistic instincts of most people. The road then follows near Yellowstone Lake. There are several hot springs in this vicinity, the thermal basin extending to the shore of the Lake, where there are such important features as *Steamboat, Butte,* and *Beach Springs.*

Continuing westward, the road passes near *Squaw Lake* (sometimes called *Indian Pond*) and finally reaches the *Fishing Bridge area.* At the *Fishing Bridge,* itself, at the outlet of Yellowstone Lake, anglers stand elbow to elbow from dawn to dusk. It was built in the summer of 1937. The first wooden bridge at the outlet to Yellowstone Lake was constructed in 1901 by the U. S. Army. Because the Lake and Fishing Bridge areas are only a few miles

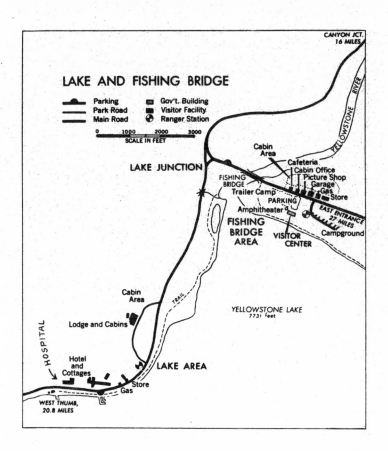

LAKE AND FISHING BRIDGE

Parking		Gov't. Building	
Park Road		Visitor Facility	
Main Road		Ranger Station	

SCALE IN FEET
0   1000   2000   3000

CANYON JCT. 16 MILES

YELLOWSTONE RIVER

LAKE JUNCTION

Cabin Area

FISHING BRIDGE

Cafeteria
Cabin Office
Picture Shop
Garage
Gas
Store

Trailer Camp

PARKING

Amphitheater

EAST ENTRANCE 27 MILES

FISHING BRIDGE AREA

VISITOR CENTER

Campground

Cabin Area

TRAIL

YELLOWSTONE LAKE 7731 feet

Lodge and Cabins

HOSPITAL

Hotel and Cottages

LAKE AREA

Store

Gas

WEST THUMB, 20.8 MILES

apart, you can participate in the naturalist programs of both. On the Storm Point walk, you explore the lake shore and swamp area, where many varieties of birds can be seen. Other walks include a three-mile climb to the crest of *Elephant Back Mountain* for a fine view of Yellowstone Lake and the Absaroka Peaks Hike which takes you above timberline to the lofty summits of the Absaroka Range. Evening campfire talks are presented each evening in both the Fishing Bridge and Bridge Bay Amphitheaters. You will also enjoy interesting exhibits of birds and other subjects in the Fishing Bridge Visitor Center.

East Gate Station to Lake Junction (26.3 miles)

Miles	Points of Interest	Miles
0.0	East Gate Station	26.3
7.3	Sylvan Pass (elevation 8,541 feet)	19.0
7.9	Lake Eleanor viewpoint	18.4
9.6	Sylvan Lake viewpoint	16.7
10.2	Teton Point. Grand Tetons viewpoint	16.1
12.6	Cub Creek crossing	13.7
16.7	*Junction.* Lake Butte road to Lake Butte and Yellowstone Lake viewpoint (0.9 mile). Trail Head 19—Thorofare trail.	9.6
19.8	Steamboat Springs	6.5
23.1	*Junction.* Squaw Lake road (0.5 mile). Indian Pond group campground.	3.2
23.3	*Junction.* Turbid Lake road. Trail Head 18—Mist Creek and Jones Pass trails start about two miles up this road.	3.0
24.5	Pelican Creek campground	1.8
24.6	Pelican Creek crossing	1.7
25.5	Fishing Bridge campground and facilities	0.8
26.0	Fishing Bridge	0.3
26.3	Lake Junction	0.0

Lake Junction to Canyon Junction (15.4 miles)

The Grand Loop Road follows the Yellowstone River along the west bank all the way. While passing through the tranquil *Hayden Valley* en route from Lake Junction to Canyon, you reach the *Mud Volcano* area. *Mud Geyser, Mud Volcano, Dragon's Mouth Spring,* and *Black Dragon's Caldron,* which is a quarter of a mile away by trail, are the most awesome in the Park. A short distance north and between the road and the Yellowstone River are several caldrons and steam vents. Chief among them is *Sulphur Caldron,* which contains large amounts of free sulphur. Short talks and conducted walks are regularly scheduled throughout the day in the Mud Volcano area, mid-June through August. There is also a fine nature trail here at the Mud Volcano.

Further along, on the west side of the Loop Road, you will be able to see the form of an ancient *Chinese Monad* depicted with unusual clarity in the meandering Trout Creek. Another stream you cross is *Alum Creek,* whose water, according to Jim Bridger, is so strong that it shrinks horses' hooves. Today, visitors who taste the waters of Alum Creek wear puckered faces long afterward because of the strong impregnation of alum.

At a point about 15 miles below the Yellowstone Lake, the river and road are forced close together by the narrowing of Hayden Valley. A little further along, the river suddenly breaks into turbulent cascades. At the point where it breaks into the first cataract, a side road leads over the *Chittenden Bridge* to *Artist Point.* Further along another side road goes to *Inspiration Point.* From either of these locations you can fully see the *Grand Canyon of Yellowstone,* truly one of the great wonders of the world. It is hard to conceive of such breathtaking beauty. The sides of this ragged pit are painted with myriads of shifting, changing, vivid colors, with shades of yellow predominating. From Artist Point it is nearly 800 feet below the platform on which you stand. Down there lies the green, serpentine *Yellowstone River.* Your gaze follows the curve of the canyon to where, in the distance, may be seen the silvery sheet of the *Lower Falls* plummeting downward in a billowy cloud of misty spray. (At Artist Point, naturalist's talks are given every half-hour through the day.) You can also see the Canyon from other angles and obtain a fuller realization of its majestic beauty. This may be done at *Point Lookout,* or farther up, at the *Grand View.*

Through foaming cataracts, the Yellowstone rushes forward to hurtle down 109 feet in a graceful fall known as the *Upper Falls.* The velocity of the flow is so great at the crest that the water pours over the lip of the canyon in a graceful arc. (A good view of the Upper Falls may be had from an observation point about one quarter mile below Chittenden Bridge.) A short distance below the Upper Falls the swift, surging torrent again comes to a mighty precipice, this time with a drop of 308 feet—the famous Lower Falls. Plunging over, it leaps downward with a thunderous roar, and disappears in a cloud of spray, presenting an unforgettable picture. A third of the fall is hidden behind this vast cloud of spray which conceals the mad play of the waters beneath. Not far from *Canyon Village* is a footpath leading to the top of the Lower Falls. The falls may also be viewed from Inspiration Point, Lookout Point, and *Red Rock Trail* (a self-guided one), which descends into the *North Rim of the Canyon.* Descriptions of other trails in this area are given on next page.

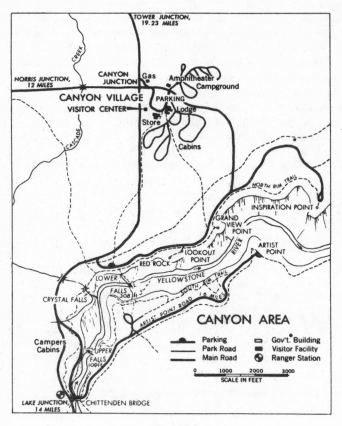

TRAILS

Name	*Miles*	*Trail Heads*	*Main Features*
Red Rock Trail	0.8	North Rim Road	Lower Falls & Grand Canyon
Lookout Point Trail	0.1	North Rim Road	Lower Falls & Grand Canyon
Inspiration Point Trail	0.1	North Rim Road	Grand Canyon
North Rim Trail	3.5	North Rim Road	Falls & Canyon
Artist Point Trail	0.2	Artist Point Road	Lower Falls & Grand Canyon
South Rim Trail	3.5	Artist Point Road	Falls & Canyon
Uncle Tom's Trail	1.0	Artist Point Road	Lower Falls, Canyon
Brink of Lower Falls Trail	0.5	North Rim Road	Lower Falls, Canyon
Brink of Upper Falls Trail	0.2	Upper Falls Road	Upper Falls

You can join the naturalist on a morning nature walk along the Canyon Rim, or an afternoon hike to *Clear Lake*. Also offered is an all-day hike to the summit of *Mount Washburn*. In addition, the Visitor Center at Canyon Village features exhibits on Yellowstone's Grand Canyon and the plants and animals that live along the Canyon's rim. A ten-minute slide program on the Canyon is presented every half hour in the auditorium. Evening campfire talks are presented each evening in the Canyon Amphitheater from early June through early September.

Miles	*Points of Interest*	*Miles*
0.0	Lake Junction	15.4
2.8	LeHardys Rapids' viewpoint	12.6
4.9	Public *emergency* roadside telephone	10.5
5.8	Mud Volcano Basin parking area	9.6
6.0	Sulphur Caldron parking area	9.4
7.7	Trout Creek crossing	7.7
9.6	Yellowstone River viewpoint	6.8
10.4	Alum Creek crossing	5.0
12.6	Otter Creek group camping area	2.8
13.1	*Junction.* Artist Point Road (1.6 miles) to Artist Point. Upper Falls drive (1 mile) at Chittenden Bridge through Canyon Rim. Trail Heads 16 (Mary Mountain trail) and 17 (Wapiti Lake trail).	2.3
14.0	*Junction.* Upper Falls drive	1.4
14.3	*Junction.* Canyon North Rim loop (3.3 miles including spur to Inspiration Point). Reenters Grand loop road at Canyon Junction.	1.1
15.4	Canyon Junction. Road to Canyon North Rim Loop and Canyon Village (0.1 mile). Road to Norris Junction (see page 45).	0.0

Canyon Junction to Tower Junction (19.2 miles)

For about 3 miles after leaving Canyon Junction, the road extends across a rolling forested country and reaches the base of Mount Washburn. Here the ascent begins that takes you through Dunraven Pass, the highest elevation (8,859 feet) that is reached on the Grand Loop Road. A few miles beyond a short service road leads to a parking area where a bus will take you to the summit of Mount Washburn. (No automobiles are permitted to make this drive because of inadequate parking space on the summit.) The panoramic view from atop this mountain is beyond description, and it is a trip that all should take.

The next point of interest along the Grand Loop is *Tower Falls,* which cannot be seen from the road. But, from a large parking area just off of it, a short path leads to the observation platform, where the 132-foot-high fall can best be seen. (For the more energetic, there is also a footpath to the bottom of the falls.) The falls gets its name from the tower-like spires, or pinnacles, of rock that guard Tower Creek's approach to the precipice. Also in this area are several excellent views of the lower end of the Grand Canyon of Yellowstone. The gorge here is approximately 500 feet deep, with almost vertical sides, and the river's waters move through the canyon as in the bottom of a trough. Along the canyon's sides, well up toward the brink, are excellent examples of columnar basalt walls (see page 18), so regular in shape that they appear to be great stone fences erected there by the hand of man.

The *Overhanging Cliffs,* just below the crossing of *Tower Creek,* overhang the road by about 40 feet for some 50 yards. A short distance beyond, a viewpoint permits you to see the *Needle,* a pinnacle that rises from the bottom of the canyon close to the edge of the water on the left bank to a height of over 250 feet. A little further along are the *Narrows,* the narrowest portion of the entire Yellowstone Canyon. In the floor of the canyon, near the Narrows, are the *Calcite Springs.* Around the fumaroles and springs in this group are deposits of gypsum as well as calcite. From the parking area here, you can see *Bumpus Butte.* As the road nears *Tower Junction* and the *Northeast Entrance road,* you pass *Roosevelt Lodge,* close to the place where President Theodore Roosevelt camped when he visited the Park.

Miles	Points of Interest	Miles
0.0	Canyon Junction	19.2
5.6	Dunraven Pass	13.6
10.6	*Junction.* Road to Mount Washburn parking area (1.2 miles)	8.6
16.6	Tower Fall parking area and road (0.5 miles) to Tower Fall campgrounds	2.6
16.8	Tower Creek	2.4
17.0	Lower Grand Canyon viewpoint	2.2
17.2	Overhanging Cliff	2.0
17.4	Needle viewpoint	1.8
17.6	Narrows parking area. View of Bumpus Butte	1.6
18.9	*Junction.* Loop road to Roosevelt Lodge (0.2 miles)	0.3
19.1	*Junction.* Loop road to Roosevelt Lodge (0.3 miles)	0.1
19.2	Tower Junction. Road to Northeast Entrance	0.0

The Northeast Entrance road lies almost wholly in the valleys of *Lamar River* and its northern tributary, *Soda Butte Creek.* The country in the valley of the Lamar River is full of interesting features, but most of them require some hiking. For instance, the *Hoodoo Basin,* near the head of *Miller Creek,* beyond the east boundary of the Park, furnishes probably the most striking example in existence of the effects of erosion and wind action upon masses of moderately soft rock. Another is *Soda Butte,* which is a singular mound of calcareous deposit built up by a now extinct hot spring. Further up, *Soda Butte Canyon* along the upper course of Soda Butte Creek is as wonderful a bit of scenery as any mountains afford. Of course, the *Lamar River Canyon* is a most remarkable gorge about a mile long, the chief characteristic of which is the enormous number and size of granite boulders that have fallen into it. The *Specimen Ridge* and the *Fossil Forests,* two points you do not want to miss, are described fully in Chapter 6.

Miles	*Points of Interest*	*Miles*
0.0	Park boundary	29.4
0.4	Entrance Ranger Station and rest rooms	29.0
6.6	Soda Butte Creek crossing	22.8
8.1	Ice Box Canyon	21.3
8.5	Trail Head 1—Thunderer cutoff trail	20.9
9.7	Pebble Creek crossing	19.7
9.9	*Junction.* Pebble Creek campground	
	road (0.8 miles) Trail Head 2—Pebble Creek trail	19.5
11.2	Trout Lake Creek crossing	18.2
13.1	Soda Butte	16.3
13.5	Trail Head 3—Lamar River trail	15.9
18.1	Rose Creek crossing	11.3
18.3	Lamar Ranger Station	11.1
23.0	*Junction.* Slough Creek road	
	to campground (3.3 miles)	6.4
23.5	Lamar River Bridge. Trail Head 4—	
	Yellowstone River trail	5.9
27.5	Junction Butte	3.9
29.4	Tower Junction	0.0

As for the interpretive programs in the area, there is a two-hour nature walk, featuring the outstanding wildflower displays along Tower Creek, scheduled several times weekly. There is also a rigorous all-day hike to the petrified forests on Specimen Ridge. Evening campfire talks are presented each evening in the Tower Fall campground from mid-June through early September.

Tower Junction to Mammoth Junction (18.1 miles)

From the Grand Loop, a short side road leads to the *Petrified Tree* (see page 124). Continuing on, *Pleasant Valley* lies north of the Loop Road. This valley is often called "Yancey's" in honor of an oldtimer in Park history, "Uncle" John Yancey, who lived in this beautiful valley and kept a crude lodging place for the convenience of visitors to this part of the Park. Driving along further, you can also see the furrowed face of *Garnet Hill* to the north. This is an Archean, Pre-Cambrian, granitic gneiss, a billion years old. Later, the valley of *Hellroaring Creek* is seen to the north side. Before reaching Mammoth, you will want to stop at *Wraith Falls* in the Lupine Creek, and the sixty-foot *Undine Falls* in the Lava Creek.

Miles	*Points of Interest*	*Miles*
0.0	Tower Junction	18.1
0.1	Tower Ranger Station	18.0
1.2	*Junction.* Petrified Tree road	
	(0.5 mile)	16.9
1.3	Yancey Creek crossing	16.8
1.5	*Junction.* Crescent Hill	
	loop road (8.2 miles)	16.6
1.8	Elk Creek crossing	16.3
3.0	Floating Island Lake viewpoint	15.1
6.4	Geode Creek crossing	11.7
7.0	Phantom Lake viewpoint	11.1
9.9	*Junction.* Crescent Hill loop road	8.2
11.2	Blacktail Deer Creek Crossing.	
	Trail Head 5—Blacktail Deer Creek trail	6.9
13.5	Wraith Falls viewpoint	4.6
13.8	Lava Creek campground	4.3
14.1	Undine Falls parking area	4.0
16.3	Gardner River Bridge	1.8
18.1	Mammoth Junction	0.0

Other Roads

While in the Park you may wish to get off the beaten path. We have already mentioned such roads as Crescent Hill loop road (formerly known as the Old Stage road or Old Tower Fall road), the Mesa road, and the Fountain Freight road. This latter one is a most pleasant detour en route from Madison Junction to Upper Geyser Basin, and one which gives a different and dramatic view of the Midway Geyser Basin and Grand Prismatic Spring.

U. S. Route 191, on its run between Bozeman and West Yellowstone, goes through the northwest corner of the Park. This road, known locally as the Gallatin Road, follows the Gallatin River and Grayling Creek valleys and offers some excellent scenery. At Specimen Creek there is a campground (see page 190). There is an excellent petrified forest near this creek, too.

In the southwest portion of the Park (the Bechler River area) a road leads from Ashton, Idaho, to the Bechler Ranger Station and Cave Falls, a distance of about 25 miles. From here the visitor has his choice of several interesting trails (see page 104). One of them takes the hiker to Old Faithful (30 miles from Bechler Ranger Station) or to the West Entrance (40 miles). There are six primitive campsites in the Bechler River Area.

MOTOR TOURS IN THE PARK

While all these drives may be enjoyed from your own automobile, the Yellowstone Park Company has available the latest in sightseeing buses and limousines. Many families that drive to the Park in their cars, board buses for the various conducted tours. The drivers, besides being experienced, are well-versed in the history and lore of Yellowstone. They thus make thoroughly competent guides, whose knowledge and experience add much to the journeys along these historic roads. The following are the major motor tours in the Park:

Mammoth. Morning tour to Tower Fall; afternoon tours to Tower Fall and Madison Junction; and evening wildlife search at 7 p.m. Contact travel desk at Mammoth Motor Inn.

Old Faithful. Tours daily to Black Sand Basin, Fountain Paint Pots, Earthquake Area, and Virginia City; and evening wildlife search at 7 p.m. Get tickets at Old Faithful Inn travel desk.

Lake. Daily in the morning to Grand Canyon (Artist Point); and evening wildlife search at 7 p.m. Get tickets at Lake Hotel travel desk.

Mount Washburn Summit Trip. Buses leave every half hour (9 a.m. to 4 p.m.) from the parking lot, taking you on an hour trip to the summit, the highest accessible point in the Park by vehicle.

PHOTOGRAPHY IN THE PARK

Yellowstone has everything for the camera addict, but the Park presents some subjects rather difficult to capture satisfactorily. Here are a half-dozen tips to keep in mind:

1. In either color or black-and-white the geysers are best photographed with quartering or slightly back light. A sky filter is almost necessary for accurate color rendering, and a yellow filter will give your black-and-white shots more interest.

2. Color shots of Old Faithful are best made very early in the morning or late in the afternoon. If you are lucky enough to catch a color shot of an eruption against a sunset sky you will have a prize.

3. Hot pools demand considerable exposure to reproduce the color in the depths of the pool. Do not waste time on hot pools if the day is cool and steam obscures the subjects. On such days the geysers give their best photographic eruptions.

4. In shooting geysers use a fast speed. Expose for the white and let the rest of the picture fall into a low key. Be sure to wipe any spray from your camera lense (and eye glasses) *immediately* since the silica residue dries very quickly and is *very* difficult to remove once it dries.

5. In using an exposure meter in Yellowstone be careful to see that bright areas in the foreground do not give a false reading.

6. If you have any questions regarding either still or moving picture photography in Yellowstone, check at one of Haynes' Photo Shops throughout the Park. Haynes' have been taking pictures in Yellowstone since 1881 when Frank Jay Haynes came to the Park. His son, Jack Ellis Haynes—often called Mr. Yellowstone—carried on until his death in 1962. Mrs. Isabel Haynes now operates the Haynes' Photo Shops.

Chapter 4.

Seeing the Grand Tetons

ALTHOUGH the two Parks are geographical neighbors, there is very little scenic similarity when you compare them. As you know, Yellowstone has its unusual attractions such as geysers, waterfalls, and bubbling hot springs. In contrast, Grand Teton is a region of mountainous grandeur, with glaciated valleys of enchanting beauty with sparkling streams and lakes.

The most imposing sight of all is the Teton Mountain range. These rugged peaks, snow-topped year 'round, form a majestic background. The dominating peak is Grand Teton which towers 7,000 feet above the valley floor. (It is this peak after which the Park takes its name.) You will find yourself thinking of the descriptive words "breathtaking beauty," and that is exactly what it is.

Besides its pinnacled peaks and majestic canyons, Grand Teton includes five large lakes and dozens of smaller bodies of water; glaciers, snowfields, and a green forest empire of pine, fir, and spruce. Much of the Park is above timberline. So, do not fail to include Grand Teton with Yellowstone (or vice versa). It will double the enjoyment of your vacation. As you can see from a glance at the map, the Jackson Hole area is just south of Yellowstone's southern border—only 6½ miles between Parks.

GEOLOGY OF THE TETONS

The Tetons are distinctive among mountains. They rise steeply more than a mile from the flat valley floor to their craggy summits. There are *no* foothills whatsoever.

Less than nine million years ago, deep and powerful pressures, perhaps partly in response to violent volcanic activity in the Yellowstone, caused a series of breaks, or faults, in the earth's crust.

71

The most spectacular of these was the *Teton Fault*. East of this earth fracture, the land sank forming the valley of Jackson Hole. To the west, lands rose creating the mountain range. Over the years vertical displacement may have totaled some 18,000 feet, but erosion has since stripped material from the Teton Range filling much of Jackson Hole so that only 7,000 feet displacement is actually visible today. The Tetons are youthful as mountains go, and occasional quakes assure us that the the Teton Fault is still active. Evidence indicates that vertical movement of over 200 feet has occurred, for example, since Jenny Lake was formed about nine thousand years ago!

The rising block was originally composed of two major rock types. An overlying layer of volcanic rock covered parts of the block. Beneath were the two more extensive formations. Of these, the upper layer—the sandstones, shales, and limestone— was deposited in seas of the Paleozoic era of geologic time. The lower crystalline rocks were formed during the first chapter of the earth's history, the Precambrian era.

As this great fault-block gradually rose with respect to the plain on the east, the volcanic rock and the sediments below it were attacked and worn down by the processes of erosion. In large areas, these rocks were stripped off entirely, exposing the ancient crystalline rocks of which most of the Teton peaks consist today. You may notice that Mount Moran, in contrast to the other Tetons, has a flat top. As you may already have guessed, Moran is still capped by sedimentary rock layers, but the processes of weathering go relentlessly on. Some day these sedimentaries, too, will be worn away; then Mount Moran may also boast the jagged type of summit so characteristic of the Teton Range.

Another distinguishing feature of Mount Moran is the long streak of black rock exposed on its face. This is a volcanic "dike":

it was formed when hot lava from below forced its way into cracks in the overlying cold rock, solidifying there before having been exposed in the flanks of Mount Moran. Grand and Middle Teton exhibit lava dikes too, but they are less conspicuous.

After the Tetons had reached their full height, glaciers of the relatively recent Ice Age crunched through stream-cut canyons, carving precipitous walls and deepening and widening their narrow floors. The debris from this process was deposited in the valley of Jackson Hole as a mass of unsorted rock and silt. On any of the trail trips into the glacial canyons among these mountains, you can see the effects of this sculpturing by ice and frost. And at the heads of such canyons you can observe where the glaciers which modified them were born—picturesque, steep-walled amphitheaters hewn into the mountainsides. These are cirques, and in each you are likely to find a lovely lake, or tarn, such as Solitude or Amphitheater Lakes, which you will surely want to visit. Small tarns are common elsewhere in the glacial canyons as well.

Many of the lakes at the foot of the Teton Mountains, such as Leigh, String, Jenny, Bradley, Taggart, and Phelps, were formed by glacial action, too. We must remember that climatic conditions were different some nine or ten thousand years ago—and more snow fell in winter than could melt in summer. Gradually it accumulated in great snowfields and glaciers. As the weight of the snow and ice increased, the ice deep within the glacier lost its firm, brittle character and began to yield and flow under the overlying weight. From the craggy mountains protruding above the snow, rocks tumbled and avalanched down onto the glacier and became part of the slow-moving river of ice. Other rock and debris was plucked and eroded along the sides and bottom of the glacier. By such action the deep U-shaped canyons were carved. (The valley of Cascade Canyon is one of nature's outstanding examples of glacial sculpturing.) As the glaciers emerged from the mountains, they spread onto the floor of Jackson Hole. There they melted, leaving a marginal rim of rocks which had been eroded from the mountains. After the glaciers disappeared, this ridge of rocks remained. Called a *moraine,* it forms a natural dam that holds back the waters of many of the piedmont or morainal lakes. Also many small, alpine lakes, hidden in the forest or deep in the Range—Suprise, Grizzly Bear, Bearpaw, Marion, Indian, Rimlock, and Holly—are the result of ice and glacial action.

The rock material left by the glacial action is of all sizes and shapes (unlike river bars where boulders are sorted and deposited according to size). The boulders here may be angular in shape. Some may show checks, flat sides, or deep grooves—evidence of the crushing weight of glaciers. The "soil" of the moraine (except

for the surface humus) is "rock flour," formed as the glacier ground and crushed small rock fragments. Actually, many things corrode the boulders and rock flour of the moraine, ultimately turning these ingredients into a true soil. Plants make the most significant contribution. Carbon dioxide is given off by growing plants, and when dissolved in rain water forms a weak acid that directly attacks rocks and minerals—finally turning them into clays. Leaves, branches, and even deeply penetrating roots die and decay, becoming humus in an ever-richer soil. Such humus is carried and mixed deeper into the moraine by burrowing animals —from tiny insects and earthworms to larger gophers and badgers. Gradually a fertile soil is formed where many new plants (which could not live on the raw glacial earth) can survive. Many of these ridge-like moraines in the Park are now beautifully forested with coniferous trees.

Some of the moraine areas in the Park, especially at higher elevations, are not forested and are good places to see samples of the different rock types of the Tetons. The hard crystalline rock of these mountains was formed by heat and enormous pressures deep within the earth's crust. Most of the Teton Range is composed of *gneiss* (a coarsely banded rock made of feldspars and quartz) and *schist* (a closely layered rock of mica and other minerals). While deeply buried within the earth, the tremendous pressure forced molten rock into many fissures and cracks. Cooled and crystallized, the light-colored veins of this once molten material became *granite*. Darker veins are *diorite*.

One of the largest enclosed valleys in the Rocky Mountains— about 60 miles north and south in length, and varied up to 12 miles in width—the floor of Jackson Hole also tells the story of glacial outwash—the glacial sand and boulders carried out of the mountains by streams. The sagebrush marks the routes of former stream flows which deposited these vast amounts of rock material on the plain even down to the banks of the Snake River and beyond. This glacial outwash deposit is too porous to support the growth of trees. But, since sagebrush is a deep-rooted shrub and is very resistant to dry conditions, it grows well on the broad level flats of Jackson Hole.

Interesting saucerlike depressions, called *potholes,* occur in the outwash plain. These are thought to be the result of recent melting of huge chunks of glacial ice that had been buried by the mantle of rock debris.

On facing page: *Grand Teton mountain range, showing Teton Glacier in foreground.*
Union Pacific Railroad Photo.

As previously stated, Jackson Hole is protected on all sides by mountains: The Tetons on the west, the high plateaus of Yellowstone on the north, the Absarokas on the northeast, the Mount Leidy Highlands on the east, the Gros Ventres on the southeast and the Hoback on the south. The southern extremity of the Tetons merges with the eastern end of the Snake River Range near the canyon where the Snake River exits from the valley.

The Park's largest river, of course, is the Snake. From the north, out of Jackson Lake, this river meanders placidly through the meadows and forests of the upper valley; then it flows more rapidly beneath steep bluffs through a series of fast riffles and quiet stretches. The Snake leaves the Park about 5 miles southwest of Park Headquarters. While the Gros Ventre River forms the southern boundary of the Park, it flows through actual Park land for only a short distance. This is also true of Buffalo Fork River in the northeastern portion of the Park.

While there is only one important river in the Park, there are many beautiful creeks and streams such as Pacific, Owl, Arizona, Berry, Spread, Pilgrim, Beaver, Taggart, Cascade Creeks. Since many of these waterways come tumbling down mountainsides, there are waterfalls such as Hidden, Twin, Glacier, Bannock, Broken, Wilderness Falls and Ribbon Cascades. But, whatever other beauties of lake, river or stream, or forest or meadow your eyes fall upon for the moment, here in Grand Teton National Park, your eyes will turn again and again to the lofty and rugged Teton Range. As you will speedily discover, no matter by which route you approach the Park, these mountains dominate the landscape.

THE ROADS OF GRAND TETON

As is true in Yellowstone, the automobile is the easiest and most popular way to see Grand Teton National Park. The Park's 245 miles of roads consist of almost every type, from narrow dirt ones to modern black top highways. Although the National Park Service avoids reference to roads as "Highways," the main road from the South Boundary of the Park to the East Boundary on Buffalo Fork (Togwotee Pass Road) most of which is new, is referred to as the "Jackson Hole Highway." This road is part of and a connecting link of U. S. Highways No. 26, 89, and 187. Formerly the "inside" road from Moose Junction past Old Headquarters and Jenny Lake to Jackson Lake Junction was the official

On facing page: *Hidden Falls, Grand Teton National Park.*
Union Pacific Railroad Photo.

connecting link in the U. S. highway system. This road is now called the "Teton Park Road."

Several old roads in the Park have been administratively determined as unnecessary to the system. These roads are marked and barred. Any road marked with a sign reading *"No Road"* is not to be used. The maximum speed permitted on most Park roads is 45 miles per hour, except where posted otherwise. The major exception is the 60 miles per hour permitted on Jackson Hole Highway. Report all accidents immediately to the nearest ranger station.

Jackson Hole Highway (South Boundary to East Boundary—28.1 miles)

The Jackson Hole Highway (U. S. Routes 26, 89, and 187) on the east side of the Snake River affords some unparalleled views of the Teton Range, heretofore enjoyed only by the rugged, venturesome visitor. The sagebrush flats are fragrant and colorful, and along the way you can catch glimpses of the Snake River, deep green between its sandy banks. The Tetons provide a gigantic backdrop for the river, the sagebrush flats, the tree-filled glacial potholes, and many small ponds. This highway actually runs from the South Boundary to the East one.

Starting at the South Boundary, which is 4½ miles from Jackson, the highway takes you along sagebrush flats on both sides. A short distance after crossing the *Gros Ventre River,* there is a junction with *Gros Ventre-Kelly road* which takes you past the improved Gros Ventre campgrounds, the town of Kelly, and on to the East Boundary line of the Park. Should you wish to drive beyond the Park's boundary on this winding dirt road, you can stop at *Gros Ventre Slide,* which permits close observation of this great rock avalanche. This slide, in 1925, ripped away a part of *Sheep Mountain,* damming the *Gros Ventre River* and forming *Slide Lake.* A rupture of this dam by high water in 1927 wiped out the town of Kelly, which has since been rebuilt.

Heading north on the Jackson Hole Highway, you can see the rugged *Gros Ventre Range* on the eastern skyline. The dominant summit is Sheep Mountain, so named because it is a favorite summer range of bighorn sheep. A little further along, on the west, you can look up into *Granite Canyon,* southernmost of the large Teton canyons. Just before reaching *Moose Junction, Blacktail Butte* can be seen on the east side of the road.

On facing page: *Snake River with Grand Tetons in background. Photograph taken at sunrise, with full moon still visible.*

Union Pacific Railroad Photo.

78

A mile or so from the Moose Junction, *Antelope Flats road* joins the highway. This dirt road, plus the *Mormon Row* and Gros-Ventre-Kelly roads which all connect to form a 10-mile loop, makes an interesting journey through the once most heavily ranched area of Jackson Hole. The flats are considered to be the dustiest, hottest, and driest area in the whole Park. The flats receive their name because the area was, at one time, a major rangeland for antelope. A few small bands still summer here.

After passing the junction with the Teton Park Road, the Jackson Hole Highway veers in a northeasterly direction. Along the way, there are several viewpoints or turnout spots that offer a dramatic scene of the magnificent Teton Range. Possibly the best of these is the *Snake River Overlook*. At about the 3½ mile point from Moose Junction, you can see, by looking toward the southeast, the livid scar of the Gros Ventre Slide on the northern portion of Sheep Mountain.

Miles	Points of Interest	Miles
0.0	South Boundary of Grand Teton National Park	28.1
0.2	*Junction.* Road to public swimming pool	27.9
2.0	Gros Ventre River crossing	26.1
2.3	*Junction.* Road to Jackson Trap Club	25.8
2.4	*Junction.* Gros Ventre-Kelly road (Gros-Ventre campground—4 miles, Kelly Post Office—7.4 miles southeast Boundary of Grand Teton National Park—11 miles to the Gros Ventre Slide—13.7 miles)	25.7
4.2	*Junction.* Road to Jackson Airport— the only one located in a national park.	23.9
8.0	MOOSE JUNCTION. Teton Park Road north to Jackson Lake Junction (see page 86)	20.1
9.2	*Junction.* Antelope Flats road	18.9
9.4	Beaver Pond viewpoint	18.7
11.4	Glacier View parking area	16.7
12.0	*Junction.* Road to picnic area	16.1
16.7	Snake River Overlook	11.4
18.5	Hedrick's Pond	9.6
20.5	*Junction.* Road to the Cunningham Homestead Cabin (0.4 miles)	7.6
21.8	Elk Post Office	6.3
22.0	Spread Creek crossing	6.1
25.8	Buffalo Fork River crossing	2.3
26.0	MORAN JUNCTION. Joins U. S. Routes 287 & 89 from the west	2.1
28.0	Moran Post Office	0.1
28.1	East Boundary of Grand Teton National Park	0.0

The Chapel of the Transfiguration.

A couple of miles beyond *Hedrick's Pond,* a short side road takes you to *Cunningham Cabin.* One of the few original homestead cabins left in Jackson Hole this is considered one of the oldest because the Cunninghams were among the first settlers in the valley. One of the most exciting events in its long history was the famous horse-thief-shooting staged here in 1893. The bullet holes in the old log cabin give it a real "wild West" atmosphere.

Nearing *Moran Junction,* you can look across the valley and see again the Tetons rise in purple grandeur from its floor. A short distance east of the Junction and you are out of the Park.

Teton Park Road (Moose Junction to Jackson Lake Junction—21.9 miles)

As you swing off U. S. Routes 26, 89, and 187 at Moose Junction, the Teton Park Road brings you into *Moose,* the headquarters of the Park. The Headquarters Building houses the *Moose Visitor Center.* This center's famous museum contains historical dioramas, exhibits, and mementos of the early fur traders (including the Colter stone), mountain men, gold prospectors, government surveyors, outlaws, and early settlers. Nearby the Visitor Center, you will find the Moose Post Office, gas station, and a fishing-tackle shop.

The *Moose-Wilson road,* joining the *Teton Park road* at Moose, is quiet and full of back-country charm. It leads southwest along moose ponds, over *Lake* and *Kaufman Creeks,* skirts the *Snake River* in places and passes several of the leading dude ranches which have made Jackson Hole a famous vacation center. Near the gate of one of these ranches, R Lazy S Ranch, is a log cabin that was the former home of Owen Wister, author of *The Virginian.* A side road off the Moose-Wilson road goes to the *Whitegrass Ranger Station.* That is, turn right 3.1 miles from Moose on the gravel road to the Whitegrass Ranch. At the ranch entrance (0.6 miles from the Wilson Road), a narrow, winding, woods road leads left to the *Whitegrass Ranger Station.*

A mile or so from Moose Junction, a short side road takes you to the parking area for the *Church of the Transfiguration* (Episcopal) and *Menor's Ferry.* The Chapel, built in 1924, is open to visitors, and services are held every Sunday morning during the summer months. The simple, rustic altar stands in front of a large picture window through which you can see the majesty of the Tetons, an offering worthy of their Creator. A short walk from the Chapel is *Menor's Ferry* (facing page). This restored ferry makes hourly crossings of the Snake, water level permitting. It is fastened to a heavy cable stretched tightly across the river and by diagonaling the ferry the swift current powers the boat across. No charge is made for the ride, which is most delightful.

While there are several viewpoints or turnouts where the Tetons are revealed in their full beauty, the *Glacier Gulch* and the *Mount Moran* ones are favorites. The former permits a full view of two of the *Three Tetons—Middle* and *Grand,* while at the latter *Mount Moran* is fully visible. At *Cathedral Group viewpoint,* you will find an extraordinary group of gigantic summits whose dominating figure is the Grand Teton. Here, in the four-mile-long area between *Avalanche* and *Cascade Canyons* are the lofty peaks of *Teewinot, Grand Teton,* and *Mount Owen.*

Menor's Ferry, originally constructed in 1892, was for thirty-five years a principal means of crossing the Snake River in Jackson Hole. Pioneers, prospectors, hunters, fishermen used it until a bridge was built in 1927 when the ferry was abandoned. Reconstructed in 1949 it is operated during summer to give visitors a chance to make a crossing like "pioneers."

83

Several trail systems start from the Teton Park Road or from nearby parking areas (see page 109). For example, both *Taggart* and *Bradley Lakes* are most easily reached from the *Lakes Trail parking area*. The trails for *Surprise* and *Amphitheater Lakes* and *Garnet Canyon* are best reached from the *Glacier Trail parking area*. To get to this parking area, drive across the small *Cottonwood Creek* bridge (downstream from the horse corrals at Jenny Lake) to *Lupine Meadows* at the base of Teewinot Mountain. Then take the dirt road, following the Glacier Trail markers, to the parking area at the end of the road.

Continuing northward, on Teton Park road, you will come to a junction with the *Jenny Lake bypass road,* which cuts out the facilities of this lake area. These include the Jenny Lake campground; gift shop; museum (geologic history of the Tetons); boat docks and launching ramp; horse concession; Exum School of American Mountaineering; Jenny Lake Ranger Station; and Jenny Lake Lodge. *Jenny Lake* is the second largest one in the Park and was named for Jenny Leigh, Shoshone wife of Richard "Beaver Dick" Leigh. The marriage of this mountain man was the first wedding ceremony with an Indian performed according to white men's law in this region. *Leigh Lake* was named in honor of Beaver Dick, and *String Lake* was once known as Beaver Dick Lake. There are several excellent trails in the area. Park naturalists conduct daily nature walks and hikes around Jenny Lake, to *Hidden Falls* and other interesting places, and give nightly campfire programs of illustrated talks or show color films.

The road up *Signal Mountain,* a little over 5 miles long, will give an enchanting view of the Teton Range, Jackson Lake, and Jackson Hole. To the east you will see *Togwotee Pass;* and to the south, the broad valley. Turnouts along the way provide picture-taking vistas, as does the lookout at the summit, 1,000 feet above the valley. You will be surveying, in those high basins around you, the birthplace of the major rivers of the west—the Snake, the Columbia, and the Missouri.

The Teton Park road ends at Jackson Lake Junction. Just before reaching this junction, you pass the *Jackson Lake Dam,* across the outlet of Jackson Lake. The old townsite of Moran was located at the foot of the dam, but was dismantled and moved 5 miles east in 1959.

On facing page: *Summer view of Snake River and Teton mountain range, seen from Oxbow Viewpoint. The major highways in Grand Teton Park offer many magnificent vistas such as this, visible from viewpoints where parking is available.* Union Pacific Railroad Photo.

Miles	Points of Interest	Miles
0.0	Moose Junction	21.9
0.4	Snake River crossing	21.5
0.6	Grand Teton National Park Headquarters and Visitor Center	21.3
0.7	*Junction.* Moose-Wilson road. Moose Post Office.	21.2
0.9	South Entrance Station	21.0
1.3	*Junction.* Road to Chapel of the Transfiguration and Menor's Ferry	20.6
2.3	Windy Point viewpoint	19.6
3.0	*Junction.* Road to Old Stewart Ranger Station (Park Headquarter's building from 1929 to 1959)	18.9
3.4	Lakes Trail parking area	18.5
3.7	Elbo Ranch	18.2
3.9	Cottonwood Creek crossing	18.0
4.8	*Junction.* Road to guest ranches and cabins	17.1
5.8	Glacier Gulch viewpoint	16.1
7.2	*Junction.* Lupine Meadows road to Jenny Lake boat launching ramp and Glacier Trail parking area.	14.7
7.5	*Junction.* Jenny Lake bypass road (4.5 miles long)	14.4
7.9	*Junction.* Road to Jenny Lake campground	14.0
9.1	Jenny Lake viewpoint	12.8
10.3	*Junction.* Road to Jenny Lake Lodge	11.6
10.5	*Junction.* Road to String Lake picnic and recreation area	11.4
11.3	Cathedral Mountain group viewpoint	10.6
13.2	*Junction.* Jenny Lake bypass road	8.7
15.5	Mount Moran viewpoint	6.4
17.5	*Junction.* Road to South Landing on Jackson Lake	4.4
18.8	*Junction.* Signal Mountain road (Jackson Lake viewpoint—2.0 miles, Jackson Point viewpoint—4.8 miles, Emma Matilda viewpoint—5.0 miles, Ranger Station—5.2 miles). Jackson Lake campground.	3.1
19.0	Signal Mountain Lodge	2.9
19.5	*Junction.* Road to Chapel of the Sacred Heart (Roman Catholic)	2.4
20.5	Jackson Lake Dam	1.4
20.8	Old townsite of Moran	1.1
21.9	Jackson Lake Lodge Junction. Routes U. S. 89 & 287 to North Boundary of Grand Teton National Park and South Entrance of Yellowstone National Park, and west to Moran Junction.	0.0

Moran Junction to Jackson Lake Junction
(U. S. Routes 89 & 287, 4.1 miles)

This road is one of the most popular in the Park. It is not only the East Entrance to the Park through *Togwotee Pass,* but it is also one of the most beautiful. *Pacific Creek* crossing is the starting point for the float trip down the Snake River to Moose. This trip is just about the ideal way to see the Park if you are a vacationer in need of a rest. Reservations for these trips are made at the Jackson Lake Lodge (see page 171 for further details).

At 1.2 mile point, the *Two Ocean Lake road* leads to the boundary line of *Teton Wilderness Area.* North on this road at about 1.8 miles the right fork follows next to Pacific Creek to Teton Wilderness boundary—7 miles from the fork. The left fork stops at *Two Ocean Lake*—2 miles from the fork. Two Ocean's sister lake, *Emma Matilda,* can only be reached from a trail that starts one mile north of the left fork.

Further along Routes 89 & 287, you will come to *Jackson Hole Wildlife Range* parking area and information center. A stop here will provide an opportunity to see a small herd of bison (buffalo). These animals, with their young, can be viewed close at hand. The range, with its exhibits and information center, is a gift of Laurance Rockefeller and the New York Zoological Society.

After passing the beautiful oxbow region of the Snake, you will soon arrive at Jackson Lake Junction. Here you can go south on the Teton Park road or north toward Yellowstone on Routes 89 & 287.

Miles	*Points of Interest*	*Miles*
0.0	Moran Junction	4.1
0.2	Buffalo (East) Entrance Station	3.9
0.4	Parking area and outdoor rest rooms	3.7
0.7	Picnic area	3.4
0.9	Pacific Creek crossing	3.2
1.2	*Junction.* Two Ocean Lake road (8.8 miles)	2.9
2.4	Parking area and information center	
	for the Jackson Hole Wildlife Range	1.7
2.9	Oxbow viewpoint	1.2
4.1	Jackson Lake Junction. U. S. Routes	
	89 & 287 goes north to Colter Bay	
	and Yellowstone National Park	
	and south to Moose via Teton Park Road.	0.0

Jackson Lake Junction to Northern Park Boundary
(U. S. Routes 89 & 287, 15.5 miles)

After swinging north on U. S. Routes 89 & 287 at Jackson Lake Junction, you will come to a side road that leads to *Jackson Lake Lodge*. This lodge is at 6,800 feet elevation, on a slight bluff over-looking *Jackson Lake* and in the lounge of the main Lodge is a spectacular 60-foot picture window framing a magnificent view of Mount Moran and its neighboring Teton peaks. Work was started on Jackson Lake Lodge in May 1953, and it was formally opened on June 12, 1955. The facility cost over six million dollars, an outright contribution of John D. Rockefeller, Jr. Complete information on facilities and accommodations at Jackson Lodge can be found in Chapter 10. Illustrated talks by naturalists are conducted on regular schedules at the Lodge, and guided nature walks leave the terrace every morning.

At *Colter Bay,* a few miles further north, there is a self-contained community providing many services for visitors. The facilities include a visitor center with information desk, auditorium, and exhibits; an outdoor amphitheater; ranger station; a trailer village; a campground; a store; a cafeteria; a grill; guest cabins; a laundry; showers; and a lakeshore marina. Each evening at Colter Bay, naturalists give illustrated talks or show color films of the Park. The subjects change nightly, and they range from "Mountaineering" to "Wildlife of the Tetons." Conducted nature walks are also given in the Colter Bay area.

Driving northward, you will note several viewpoints or turn-outs at which you can look at the shoreline of Jackson Lake, with the Teton Range as a backdrop. It is the largest of the several glacial-made lakes in the Park and is the second largest natural lake in Wyoming. (Yellowstone Lake is the largest.) Jackson Lake has a shoreline of approximately 52 miles containing 25,730 acres. It is as deep as 400 feet and is over 10 miles long. The lake was enlarged to its present size in 1916 by a dam at the outlet which increased the water level 39 feet and the length 5 miles. As summer progresses Jackson begins to have even more prominent shore-lines marked by cobbles, dead snags, and stumps—quite unlike Jenny and Leigh Lake shorelines where forest trees grow to the water's edge. This is explained by the annual drawdown of water

On facing page: *One of the best ways to see the Parks is by trail, such as this in Cascade Canyon. Grand Teton and Mt. Owen peaks are visible in the far distance.*
Grand Teton Lodge Company Photo.

at Jackson Lake Dam, which creates an area of fluctuating water levels and does not allow vegetation to become established.

The common boundary between Grand Teton National Park and Teton National Forest is reached some 15½ miles from Jackson Lake Junction. If you continue along this road 6½ more miles you will reach the South Entrance of Yellowstone National Park.

Miles	Points of Interest	Miles
0.0	Jackson Lake Junction	15.5
0.5	*Junction.* Road to Jackson Lake Ranger Station	15.0
0.6	*Junction.* Road to Jackson Lake Lodge	14.9
2.5	Pilgrim Creek crossing	13.0
4.8	*Junction.* Colter Bay road to major visitor's area, accommodations, boat launching ramp, and Visitor Center	10.7
5.7	*Junction.* Road to Leek's Lodge	9.8
9.8	Arizona Creek crossing	5.7
10.3	Arizona Creek Ranger Station	5.2
10.8	Jackson Lake shoreline viewpoint	4.7
13.0	Lizard Creek crossing	2.5
13.6	*Junction.* Road to Lizard Point campground	1.9
15.5	North Boundary of Grand Teton National Park. (North 6.5 miles to South Entrance of Yellowstone National Park)	0.0

One of the most interesting and easy ways of seeing Grand Teton National Park is to take a boat-bus tour. This six-hour trip by bus and boat visits every key interest point in the Park—for cameras, sightseeing views, and wildlife. An unexcelled narrative of historical lore, geology, and wildlife by a driver native to Jackson Hole and the Tetons is given throughout the tour. The boat cruise on Jackson Lake, with lunch on Elk Island, is the highlight of the trip.

PICTURE MAKING AND PICTURE TAKING

Grand Teton National Park is an ideal place for the artist or photographer. Inasmuch as a camera is a standard item in any family's vacation equipment, we assume you will bring one with you. But you might be alerted to bring a telephoto lens (for the mountains, birds, and mammals), or a wide-angle or a portrait lens if you are interested in photographing flowers.

Use a skylight or haze filter to cut out harmful ultraviolet light which is much stronger at this high elevation than at sea level. A pola-screen is even better and will give dramatic sky tones. Exposure meters are just as accurate here as at sea level and we recommend their use for the best results. If you do not have an exposure meter, follow the data sheet packed with every roll of film. But with or without an exposure meter, it is wise to shoot two or three different exposures of the same subject. Mountain light is deceiving.

Exposed film should be developed as soon as possible and not left in glove compartments or closed cars. Heat damages any film, particularly color and Polaroid film. Photographic concessioners at Jenny Lake and Jackson Lake Lodge have ample supplies of film on hand and will help you with any special photographic problem. Artist's supplies are available at Jenny Lake Studio.

Picture viewpoints or turnouts in both Grand Teton and Yellowstone are provided by the National Park Service. They afford the best places to pull off the road and stop in safety to look at the view, make sketches, or take photos.

Chapter 5.

Seeing the Parks
on Foot or by Horseback

FROM the Parks' road system a vast panorama of scenery is revealed, and with luck some wildlife also may be observed, particularly during the early morning and evening. For a more intimate contact with this wonderful region, the trails of both Parks offer many new and interesting experiences. Actually, the scenery of the "back country" is a living museum of nature.

Trail riding and hiking offer the best means of full enjoyment of the wilderness back country. Horses are available in both Parks at the following locations:

Yellowstone National Park. You can rent horses at Mammoth Hot Springs, Canyon, Roosevelt, and Old Faithful. These are scheduled trips to specific destinations; none may be made without a guide. You can, however, make up your own guided party and spend a day or several days exploring some of the wonderful trails through arrangements with dude ranchers or licensed guides in the vicinity of the Park. For information on these, write to the Dude Ranchers Association, P. O. Box 1363, Billings, Montana 59101, or Wyoming Outfitters Association, Afton, Wyoming.

Grand Teton National Park. Strings of horses at Jenny Lake, Jenny Lake Lodge, Jackson Lake Lodge, and Colter Bay corrals provide mounts for almost every class of horsemanship. There are guided trail rides of one to three hours' duration, day guided

On facing page: *Horseback riding on trail near Jenny Lake, Grand Teton.*
Grand Teton Lodge Company Photo.

trips, overnight junkets, and pack trips. (Horses are available without a guide to competent riders only.) There are also breakfast and wrangler steak supper rides, in which cowboy-cooked food is served to satisfy any cowboy appetite. Moonlight and campfire rides are sometimes available at the various corrals within the Park.

On overnight and pack trips, your wrangler will provide sleeping equipment (tents and sleeping bags) and food, and you will find that your guide not only knows all about horses, but turns a mean flapjack as well. On the day trips, you furnish and pack your own lunch. If you are staying at a guest ranch, horses will be furnished and pack trips arranged by your host. Otherwise, contact Teton Trail Rides at Jenny Lake for pack-trip rates, or write to the Jackson Hole Chamber of Commerce (see page 188 for address) for information on outfitters and guides who come into the Park.

THE PARKS' BACK COUNTRY

Riders and hikers will find they can spend hours, days, or even weeks in Yellowstone-Teton country. The trails mentioned in this chapter are in good condition. But even an excellent trail may be blocked off to hikers by impassable fords during high water. Therefore, be sure to get the latest trail condition data from district Park Ranger before leaving for the back country.

YELLOWSTONE'S WILDERNESS TRAILS

Only a small percentage of the Park is developed (roads, villages, campgrounds). Thus, from almost any point along the busy Grand Loop Road, you may walk 300 yards and feel completely detached from anything manmade. There, in the quiet of forest or meadow, the buzzing of a fly or a mosquito or the song of a bird is a dominating sound.

The Park offers you several hundred miles of well-marked back-country trails. The Howard Eaton Trail, named after the famous horseman and guide, parallels roughly the Grand Loop Road for some 150 miles. It is a horseback trail, but it may be hiked as well. But, before starting out on back-country trails, you should review plans with a ranger to check on current trail conditions. All of the following trails are marked along the way

On facing page: *Jenny Lake and Grand Tetons in background.*
Union Pacific Railroad Photo.

Name	Approx. Miles Length	Trail Heads	Principal Features
Northwest Corner:			
Daly Creek Trail	10.0	Trail Head 8, Gallatin Road	Bighorn Peak and Gallatin Petrified Forest
Lava Butte Trail	2.5	Reached via Daly Cr. Trail	Lava Butte
Bighorn Peak Trail	10.0	Gallatin Road at Black Butte Creek	Bighorn Peak
High Lake Loop Trail	10.0	Reached via Sportsman Lake Trail	High, Sedge, Crag and Crescent Lakes
Sportsman Lake Trail	24.0	Mammoth and Trail Head 9, Gallatin Road	Sportsman Lake and Gallatin Mountains
Mol Heron Trail	3.0	Reached via Sportsman Lake Trail	Connecting trail to Mol Heron Creek Road
Fawn Pass Trail	25.0	Trail Head 10 on Gallatin Road and via Sportsman Lake Trail	Gallatin Range
Bighorn Pass Trail	25.0	Trail Head 11 on Gallatin Road or Indian Creek Campground	Gallatin Mountains

by orange metal tags on trees or posts. Mileage location of the various trail heads that start from the Grand Loop Roads are given in Chapter 3.

Northwest Corner. This area includes the Gallatin Range of mountains and the surrounding country from which flow those headwater streams feeding the Gardner River on the east and the Gallatin and Madison Rivers on the west. The Gallatin Range is only about 20 miles long. The highest point in the Gallatins is Electric Peak (10,992 feet). It stands at the northern end of the range. Mount Holmes designates the southern terminus of these mountains and is 10,336 feet in elevation. Seventeen other peaks are scattered from north to south between these two. As

Name	Approx. Miles Length	Trail Heads	Principal Features
Northwest Corner:			
West Boundary Trail	10.0	Gallatin Ranger Sta.	West Boundary
Gneiss Creek Trail	16.0	Trail Head 12 on West Entrance Rd.	Edge of Madison Valley
Cougar Creek Trail	24.0	U. S. 191 at Madison Bridge	Lodgepole Pine Country
Mount Holmes Trail	11.0	Trail Head 13 on Grand Loop Road	Summit Mt. Holmes
Grizzly Lake Trail	5.0	Grand Loop Road at Obsidian Creek	Grizzly Lake
Bunsen Peak Trail	5.0	Mammoth or Golden Gate	Summit Bunsen Peak
Sepulcher Mountain Trail	4.0	Mammoth	Summit Sepulcher Mtn.
Beaver Pond Trail	5.0	Mammoth	Aspen and Beaver Ponds on flanks of Sepulcher Mtn.
Purple Mountain Trail	3.0	Near Madison Jct.	Summit Purple Mtn.

you enter the area, either from the east or west, these peaks are a cool and beautiful invitation to the wilderness visitor.

Four main trails lead from east to west across the Gallatin wilderness. These trails provide general access to the entire area. Several lesser ones lead to specific sections. Much of the crest of the range lies above treeline, or in the subalpine meadows interspersed with clumps of trees where cross-country travel is comparatively easy. As this high country is the summer home of large numbers of wild animals such as deer, elk, and bighorn sheep, you will probably spend considerable time off the trails photographing and observing them. Nowhere can wildlife photographers get pictures with more natural and beautiful backgrounds than here. Fishing is also fine in this area and you can find many good campsites along the creeks en route.

Washburn-Buffalo Plateau Area

Name	Length Miles	Trail Heads	Principal Features
Yellowstone River Trail	23.5	Gardiner and Trail Head 4	Black Canyon of the Yellowstone R.
Rescue Creek Trail	7.0	Trail Head 7, North Entrance Rd.	Mount Everts
Blacktail Deer Creek Trail	5.0	Trail Head 5, Grand Loop Road	Blacktail Deer Creek and Yellowstone River
Crevice Trail	3.0	Reached via Yellowstone R. Trail	Crevice Creek
Hellroaring Trail	6.0	Reached via Yellowstone R. Trail	Hellroaring Creek
Coyote Creek Trail	4.0	Reached via Yellowstone R. Trail	Coyote Creek
Buffalo Plateau Trail	15.0	Reached via Slough Creek or Yellowstone R. Trail	Buffalo Plateau
Garnet Hill Trail	4.5	Tower Ranger Station	Access to Hell-roaring Creek and Yellowstone River
Slough Creek Trail	12.0	Slough Creek Campground Road	Slough Creek
Pebble Creek Trail	12.0	Trail Head 2 and at Warm Creek on NE Entrance Road	Pebble Creek
Elk Tongue Trail	5.5	Reached via Pebble Creek Trail	Elk Tongue Creek
Solfatara Creek Trail	8.0	Norris Campground	Solfatara Creek
Ice Lake Trail	0.3	Norris-Canyon Cutoff-Road	Ice Lake
Grebe Lake Trail	3.0	Trail Head 15, Norris-Canyon Cutoff	Grebe Lake
Cascade Lake Trail	3.0	Norris-Canyon Cutoff-Road	Cascade Creek and Lake
Mount Washburn Trail	5.0	Dunraven Pass	Summit Mount Washburn

Washburn-Buffalo Plateau Area. Three major creeks originate and flow north to the Yellowstone River from this area. They are Lava, Blacktail Deer, and Tower Creeks. Hellroaring and Coyote Creeks flow into the Yellowstone from the north. The Washburn Range extends north and south through almost the center of the area. Much of the lower parts are open sagebrush-grassland. Deeply worn migration trails used by elk in spring and autumn lead through the forests over the Washburn Range and on toward Central Plateau to the south. These are invitations to the backpack camper to strike off the road and keep going.

Central Plateau Area. It was through this area in 1877 that the Nez Percé Indians under Chief Joseph were pursued by the United States Army under General Howard. Encroachment upon their land (which lay west of the Rocky Mountains) by white settlers, and the subsequent attack upon them by the white man in an endeavor to force them to a reservation, brought about their retreat into western Montana and across Yellowstone Park. From here they planned on reaching the eastern buffalo grounds. En route they had three battles with the troops which had been sent against them. It was while in this Central Plateau area that some of the wilder young braves captured a group of tourists. The tense situation broke down when several of the tourists made a break for the woods. As a result, George Cowan, the leader of the tourist party, was shot and left for dead—though he did survive. Those tourists who did not run away were released at the Mud Volcano, when the Indians crossed the Yellowstone and headed northeast. As you hike in this area you may find the campsite of the Cowan party near the Fountain Paint Pot area and the place where George Cowan was shot at the foot of Mary Mountain on Nez Percé Creek.

Name	Approx. Length Miles	Trail Heads	Principal Features
Central Plateau Trail	12.0	Trail Head 14 Norris-Canyon Cutoff	Cygnet Lakes; Central Plateau
Mary Mountain Trail	20.0	Trail Heads 25 & 16	Nez Percé; Hayden Valley; Mary Lake
Mallard Lake Trail	4.5	Trail Head 24, Old Faithful Area	Mallard Lake

Northeast Corner

Name	Approx. Length Miles	Trail Heads	Principal Features
Northeast Corner:			
Specimen Ridge Trail	16.0	NE Entrance Road near Junction Butte	Fossil Forest; Amethyst Mountain
Lamar River Trail	25.0	Trail Head 3, NE Entrance Road	Lamar River; Absaroka Range
Cache Creek Trail	17.0	Reached via Lamar River Trail	Cache Creek; Absaroka Range
Thunderer Cutoff Trail	7.5	Trail Head 1, NE Entrance Road	The Thunderer
Miller Creek Trail	16.0	Reached via Lamar River Trail	Miller Creek; Absaroka Range; Hoodoo Basin
Canoe Lake Trail	4.0	Reached via Miller Creek Trail	Canoe Lake; Absaroka Range
Bootjack Gap Trail	4.0	Reached via Miller Creek Trail	Absaroka Range
Frost Lake Trail	6.0	Reached via Lamar River Trail	Absaroka Range
Mist Creek Pass Trail	19.0	Trail Head 18, East Entrance Road	Pelican Valley; Mist Pass

Northeast Corner. Bounded by the Absaroka Mountains on the east and the Yellowstone River on the west, this is a unique wilderness area. Fossil forests, large thermal areas, a goodly part of the Grand Canyon of the Yellowstone, an abundant and varied wildlife, fishing, and mountain scenery are all to be found in this one roadless tract.

Northeast Corner

Name	Approx. Length Miles	Trail Heads	Principal Features
Northeast Corner:			
Wapiti Lake Trail	25.0	Trail Head 17, Chittenden Bridge	Wapiti Lake; Upper Pelican Creek
Fern Lake Trail	7.7	Reached via Wapiti Lake Trail	Fern Lake
Astringent Creek Trail	8.0	Reached via Mist Creek Pass Trail	White and Tern Lakes; Astringent Creek
Pelican Cone Trail	4.5	Reached via Mist Creek Pass Trail	Summit Pelican Cone
Jones Pass Trail	7.0	Trail Head 18, East Entrance Road	Absaroka Range
Ribbon Lake Trail	3.5	Artist Point Parking Area	Ribbon Lake
Clear Lake Trail	1.0	Uncle Tom's Trail Parking Area	Clear Lake
Seven Mile Hole Trail	7.0	North Rim Drive	Grand Canyon of Yellowstone

Easily accessible by a number of trails, most of which are on easy grades, you can cross the entire area from north to south in two days. The meadows here are large and make good places to camp and you can again catch trout in any of the many streams. A herd of bison is usually seen in the high country for this corner of the Park is one of their favorite summer ranges.

Southeast Corner

Name	Approx. Length Miles	Trail Heads	Principal Features
Southeast Corner of Park:			
Thorofare Trail	33.0	Trail Head 19, East Entrance Rd.	Yellowstone Lake Upper Yellowstone River
Heart Lake Trail	30.0	Trail Head 21, So. Entrance Rd.	Heart Lake; Heart Lake Geyser Basin; South and Southeast Arm Yellowstone Lake
Clear Creek Trail	9.5	Sylvan Lake, East Entrance Rd.	Clear Creek
Mountain Creek Trail	9.0	Reached via Thorofare Trail	Mountain Creek; Eagle Pass
South Boundary Trail	36.0	South Entrance Station	Headwaters of Snake River
Big Game Ridge Trail	8.0	Reached via South Boundary Trail	Big Game Ridge

Southeast Corner. This is a big area, and to make an extended trip into it, you should do so with pack and saddle horses. However, hikers can easily make shorter trips into this country starting from several points. The length of the trip depends only upon the individual's physical strength and enthusiasm. In any case the trip will be well worth while. In this area you can enjoy a canoe, horseback, or back-pack trip into a wonderful wilderness. It can be classed "big league," as primitive areas go.

102

Name	Approx. Length Miles	Trail Heads	Principal Features
Southeast Corner of Park:			
Red Creek Trail	9.0	Reached via South Boundary Trail	Red Creek; Basin Lake; Sheridan Lake
Mount Sheridan Trail	4.0	Reached via Heart Lake Trail	Summit Mount Sheridan
Basin Creek Trail	3.0	Reached via South Boundary Trail	Basin Creek
Heart River Trail	3.0	Reached via South Boundary Trail	Heart River
Riddle Lake Trail	2.5	Trail Head 22, So. Entrance Road	Riddle Lake
Chipmunk Creek Trail	18.0	Reached via South Boundary Trail	Two Ocean Plateau
Snake River Look-out	2.0	South Entrance Station—Trail Head 20	Slopes of Huckle-berry Mountain

This area is the summer home of many elk. Members of both the Northern Yellowstone and the Jackson Hole elk herds summer in the Upper Yellowstone and Snake River regions. A favorite route for many pack trips originating at South Entrance leads up the Snake River to Red Creek, and then up Red Creek on the Heart Lake Trail to Heart Lake. There are good trout in this lake, but sometimes they do not cooperate with the angler. The best lake in the area for cutthroat trout seems to be Basin Creek Lake.

103

Name	Approx. Length Miles	Trail Heads	Principal Features
Southwest Corner:			
Old Fountain Trail	13.0	Trail Head 12 and Fountain Freight Road	Madison Plateau
Fairy Creek Trail	3.0	Biscuit Basin and Fountain Freight Road	Fairy Creek; Fairy Falls
Summit Lake Trail	13.0	Biscuit Basin	Madison Plateau; Summit Lake
Fern Cascades Trail	2.0	Old Faithful	Fern Cascades
West Boundary Trail	36.0	Bechler Ranger Station and West Yellowstone	Madison Plateau
Bechler River Trail	32.0	Bechler Ranger Station and Lone Star Geyser Road	Bechler Meadows; Bechler River; and many waterfalls
Boundary Creek Trail	12.5	Reached via Bechler River Trail	Dunanda Falls; Buffalo Lake
Bechler Falls Trail	4.5	Cave Falls Road	Bechler Falls

Southwest Corner. This area includes the whole Cascade Corner of the Park and the Madison and Pitchstone Plateaus as well. This is a large, roadless country, about 35 miles long and averaging some 18 miles or so in width. A great variety of wilderness trips may be taken here by horseback, back-pack, or canoeing. The Bechler River is on the Pacific slope, and the Cascade Corner has a somewhat warmer and moister climate than does most of the

Southwest Corner

Name	Approx. Length Miles	Trail Heads	Principal Features
Southwest Corner:			
South Boundary Trail	20.0	Bechler Ranger Station	Winegar, South Boundary and Tanager Lakes
Old Marysville Road	11.0	Grassy Lake Road or reached via Bechler River Trail	Mountain Ash Creek and Falls River
Union Falls Trail	2.0	Reached via Old Marysville Road Trail	Union Falls
Pitchstone Plateau Trail	17.0	South Entrance Road	Pitchstone Plateau
Beula Lake Trail	2.0	Grassy Lake Road	Beula Lake
Shoshone Lake Trail	24.0	Trail Head 23 on Grand Loop Road	Shoshone Lake and Geyser Basin
The Channel Trail	7.0	South Entrance Road	Shoshone Lake Outlet Channel
Dogshead Trail	4.0	South Entrance Road	Shoshone Lake
Divide Lookout Trail	1.9	Grand Loop Road near Craig Pass	Continental Divide

rest of the Park. This climatic difference might not be noticeable to you, but it is sufficient to let somewhat more succulent vegetation grow. The huckleberries are more plump and juicy, and the aspen trees between the Bechler River Ranger Station and the Bechler Meadows are larger and straighter than those found in drier parts of the Park.

ALONG TETON TRAILS

There are over 200 miles of trails in the Park, some leading to high mountain lakes and passes above timberline, others through the valley. Perhaps the best get-acquainted hike is the half-day trip to Hidden Falls. It has the added attraction that it can begin and end with a boat trip across Jenny Lake; the falls are only half a mile from the landing on the farther shore. You will do well to join the naturalist's party at the museum the first time you go, for he will tell you much that will serve as a background for visiting other sections of the park.

Whether you are an experienced hiker of mountain trails or a novice, never travel alone; accustom yourself gradually to hiking and climbing. The better known trails are:

The Lakes Trail. This leads along the mountain base from Phelps Lake to Jackson Lake and passes along the shores of Taggart, Bradley, Jenny, String, and Leigh Lakes. The path takes you for the most part along shady, wooded ridges.

Glacier Trail. Part of this overlaps the Lakes Trail, from the boulder field south of Jenny Lake into the woods. Then it leaves the low country and takes you up the east slope of the Grand Teton to Surprise and Amphitheater Lakes. The last-named is the starting point for the climb to Teton Glacier.

Cascade Canyon Trail. From the south end of Jenny Lake, you hike to Hidden Falls and ascend the canyon between towering peaks. Steady going brings you to the fork of the trail—the north branch leads to Lake Solitude, the south to Alaska Basin. From this basin, seeing the range from the western slope gives you a feeling of discovery, and it gives added meaning to the geological story.

Lake Solitude, in its alpine setting among the peaks, is one of several high-country goals for hikers. On the other hand, Alaska Basin is less frequented because of its greater distance. Those who complete this fairly ambitious hike are rewarded in season by the most dazzling wildflower display to be found anywhere in the Park.

Skyline Trail. This trail is a fine high trail along the crest of the Teton Range. You may shortcut the 25-mile Skyline Trail by taking the boat trip across Jenny Lake to enter Cascade Canyon, then travel up Cascade to the fork, thence up the South Fork and over Hurricane Pass into Alaska Basin. Continue along the Skyline west of Buck Mountain to Static Peak, and then on to the Whitegrass Ranger Station. This trail may be covered in one day by a seasoned hiker.

106

Paintbrush Trail. From the south end of Leigh Lake this trail climbs to the upper end of Paintbrush Canyon, colorful as its name. A heavy snow accumulation remains on the upper sections of this trail throughout most of the summer, making the climb to the Paintbrush divide a hazardous undertaking unless the hiker is equipped with ice axe and rope. The hike over the divide to Lake Solitude and the similar trip from Lake Solitude over the divide into Paintbrush Canyon are recommended to the average hiker only from early August until September, owing to the danger in crossing the steep snowfields and icefields in that area. Actually, the trip to Lake Solitude via Paintbrush Canyon and return by Cascade Canyon is one of the more popular and beautiful overnight hikes in Grand Teton National Park.

From Phelps Lake, the *Death Canyon Trail* to Alaska Basin, and the *Open Canyon Trail* to Marion Lake offer spectacular vistas to the hiker or the horseman. *Granite Canyon Trail* is another interesting trail in the same general area. Although the trails are well marked, they are recommended only to hikers with considerable endurance.

If traveling to one of the dude ranches south of the Park near the Moose-Wilson road, you may turn right (south) near the inlet of Phelps Lake and take the new Phelps Lake Trail to the Wilson road parking area. This trail is a spur which branches from the Granite-Open Canyons Trail. It traverses coniferous forest and terminates at the Wilson road parking area.

Another interesting trail is the one to Garnet Canyon. From the Glacier Trail, a 1.2-mile spur traverses into Garnet Canyon and ends in a boulder field on the canyon floor. Though the boulders are the end of the officially maintained trail an indistinct path continues to the caves above Spaulding Fall. Travel beyond the boulder field is prohibited unless hikers have registered (see page 115). The Garnet Canyon Trail is used chiefly by mountaineers en route to the Three Tetons.

The most popular trails in Grand Teton National Park are those originating at Jenny Lake. Most hikers prefer to park at the Jenny Lake Visitor Center or campground; then either hike around the south end of Jenny or eliminate 2.4 miles of walking by taking a boat to the west shore. Though starting from the visitor center is often the most convenient, the parking area at the lower end of String Lake affords better access to all trails in the Jenny Lake section and is 0.7 miles shorter. From there, Cascade Canyon may be approached by the more scenic northwest shore of Jenny Lake along an excellent trail that has far less use by horses than the trails from the visitor center.

Distances

Jenny Lake Visitor Center TO:

Around Jenny Lake	7.1	miles
Lupine Meadows	2.0	
Garnet Canyon	7.2	
Surprise Lake	7.5	
Amphitheater Lake	8.0	
Hidden Falls	2.7 *	
Forks of Cascade Canyon	6.6 *	
Cascade Ranger Station	7.0 *	
Hurricane Pass (10,600 feet)	11.8 *	
Alaska Basin	13.5 *	
Buck Mountain Divide (10,550 feet)	17.4 *	
Death Canyon Ranger Station	20.9 *	
Whitegrass Ranger Station	25.0 *	(via Skyline Trail)
Whitegrass Ranger Station	10.1	(via Lakes Trail)
Lake Solitude	9.3 *	
Paintbrush Divide (10,645 feet)	11.4 *	(via Cascade Canyon Trail)
Holly Lake	14.6	(via Cascade & Paintbrush Divide)
String Lake	19.5	(via Cascade & Paintbrush Divide)
Jenny Lake Loop	25.9	(via Cascade & Paintbrush Divide)
String Lake	3.2	
Holly Lake	10.1	(via Paintbrush Trail)
Paintbrush Divide	12.6	(via Paintbrush Trail)
Leigh Lake	4.5	

String Lake Picnic Area TO:

Around String Lake	3.6	miles
Outlet of Leigh Lake	1.0	
North end of Leigh Lake	4.6	
Bearpaw Lake	5.1	
Holly Lake	6.4	
Paintbrush Divide	8.2	
String Lake Loop	19.5	(via Cascade Canyon & Paintbrush Trails)
Hidden Falls	2.2	
Jenny Lake Visitor Center	3.2	

* By boat across Jenny Lake reduces trail's distance by 2.4 miles.

108

Glacier Trail Parking Area TO:

Surprise Lake	5.4	miles
Amphitheater Lake	5.6	
Garnet Canyon	4.8	

Lakes Trail Parking Area TO:

Whitegrass Ranger Station	5.0	miles
Taggart Lake	1.3 *	
Bradley Lake	2.0	
Garnet Canyon	5.5	
Surprise Lake	8.6	
Amphitheater Lake	9.0	
Lupine Meadows	7.2	
Jenny Lake	8.8	

Whitegrass Ranger Station TO:

Phelps Lake	2.2	miles
Mount Hunt Divide (9,700 feet)	7.5	
Granite Canyon Patrol Cabin	11.0	
Marion Lake	12.9	(via Open-Granite Canyons)
Marion Lake	11.8	(via Death Canyon Trail)
Death Canyon Ranger Station	4.1	
Phelps Lake Overlook	7.0	
Buck Mountain Divide	7.6	
Alaska Basin	11.5	
Hurricane Pass	13.2	
Cascade Trail Junction	18.5	
Jenny Lake	25.0	(via Skyline Trail)
Taggart Lake	4.1	
Bradley Lake	5.2	
Lupine Meadows	8.1	
Jenny Lake	10.1	(via Lakes Trail)

Colter Bay Area TO:

Colter Bay Self-Guiding Nature Trail (loop)	1.8	miles (Starts behind Colter Bay Visitor Center—foot trail only)
Hermitage Point Trail (loop)	8.8	(Starts—corrals at Colter Bay cabin area)

Jackson Lake Horse Area TO:

Around Christian Pond	4.8	miles
Around Emma Matilda Lake	10.8	
Around Two Ocean Lake	12.2	
Around both lakes	14.2	
To Wildlife Range and return	4.4	

* Three miles to lake via Taggart Creek and return via Beaver Creek.

Berry Creek-Webb Canyon

The Berry Creek-Webb Canyon Country in the northwest corner of the Park is very interesting, but seldom traveled. A few unmarked secondary trails lead into this country. Generally, they are trails maintained by park rangers on their fire patrols. These trails begin at Berry Creek Ranger Station near the upper west shore of Jackson Lake. This ranger station is accessible by boat, one-half mile from the Lizard Point campground, or by horseback, from Dime Creek in the Teton National Forest via an unmarked, indistinct trail leading south and fording the Snake River. Upper Berry Creek is also accessible to hikers from the Hominy Lookout road, a Forest Service unimproved road from Ashton, Idaho.

Berry Creek Ranger Station TO:

Targhee National Forest Boundary	10.2 miles (via Conant Trail)
Mouth of Owl Creek	3.2
Moose Basin Divide	10.2 (via Owl Creek Trail)
Lower Moose Basin	6.1 (via Webb Canyon Trail)
Moose Basin Divide	10.0 (via Webb Canyon Trail)

A few visitors prefer to do off-trail hiking. Such hikers must sign out and in, and should travel in a party. The hikers must display to the district ranger some knowledge of hiking in the conditions he may find. For example, many of the Park's back-country areas have steep snowbanks which require an ice axe. An ice axe is a dangerous tool in inexperienced hands, and if the hiker does not know how to use one he should not hike in areas where one is needed. The rangers at the various signing-out stations will gladly make suggestions. The popular off-trail hikes in the Park are: Rimrock Lake, Avalanche Canyon, Teton Glacier, Hanging Canyon, Leigh and Moran Canyons, and Wilderness Falls. Often a party will simply want to get high on the mountains, get off the main trails for awhile. Laurel Lake and Hanging Canyon are good suggestions.

110

APPROVED BACK-COUNTRY CAMPSITES

As in Yellowstone, back-country visitors in Grand Teton National Park must have a campfire permit in their possession if they wish to build a fire, and they must build fires only in established places at approved campfire sites. Campfire permits may be used for the following back-country campsites in Grand Teton:

Site Number	*Location*
1	Berry Creek Meadows
2	Beach at Warm Springs on Jackson Lake
3	Outlet of Two Ocean Lake
4	Moran Bay—Near Moran Creek
5	Elk Island—Northeast Beach
6	South Landing on Jackson Lake
7	Spalding Bay on Jackson Lake
8	Beach west of Leigh Lake Patrol Cabin
9	Beach at end of old road to Leigh Lake
10	Beach near center of east shore on Leigh Lake
11	Beach on southwest shore of Leigh Lake
12	First Lake in Leigh Canyon
13	Holly Lake
14	Lake Solitude
15	Hanging Canyon (Ramshead Lake or Lake of the Crags)
16	Near forks of Cascade Creek
17	Upper south fork of Cascade Creek
18	Surprise or Amphitheater Lakes
19	Garnet Canyon (platforms or meadows)
20	Outlet of Bradley Lake
21	Southeast shore of Taggart Lake, near outlet
22	Alaska Basin
23	Death Canyon Bench
24	Marion Lake
25	Death Canyon (one mile west of Ranger Station)
26	Granite Canyon (near Patrol Cabin)
27	North end of Phelps Lake
28	On road just before reaching Whitegrass Ranger Station

Overnight camping will be permitted on the Snake River for boaters *only* and then at sites other than those listed as picnic areas (see page 194).

BACK-COUNTRY ETIQUETTE
AND REGULATIONS

A party desiring to make either a horseback or hiking trip into the back country, on their own without benefit of a guide, must do the following:

1. Go to a ranger station and obtain a campfire permit for the area or areas they will be in.
2. Give their itinerary to the ranger. This is necessary for several reasons, including protection of the visitor and the protection of the Park. Never hike alone.
3. Always report the completion of your trip to prevent a needless search, and turn in the campfire permit at the same time.

Anybody going into the back-country should by all means obtain a topographic map of the Park that you are in and should have a compass. You must know how to use them to avoid becoming lost or getting into difficult situations requiring the help of a rescue party. Obtain a topographic map of the Park from the Geological Survey, U. S. Department of the Interior, Washington, D. C., 20240, or at one of the museums in the Park (see page 202). A good compass, such as the Silva with an azimuth face on which the magnetic declination can be set off, is preferable to the small pocket-type.

In addition, keep the following back-country etiquette and regulations in mind:

1. In general, there are several things that you may do as a camper or hiker to conserve the wild beauty of the Yellowstone-Teton Country. First, in choosing a campsite, pick one that already has the scar of an old campfire and build your fire there. If you are traveling with stock, unpack at your campsite, and then hobble your horses well away from campsites, lakes, and trails.
2. When making camp, do not "ditch" your tent or dig a level area. These scars last several years, even if the soil is carefully replaced (and no two parties have the same-size tents). Of course, cutting fir boughs for beds has long been a poor practice.
3. Sanitation at high campsites is a tougher problem. There is literally no place left to bury cans and foil. Marmots have invariably become civilized enough to dig up such refuse. Burn that which is flammable, and then pack out your flattened cans and foil with you. For personal sanitation, walk well away from campsites, trails, and streams and bury all human waste.

4. For campfires, you may gather only wood that is dead and fallen to the ground. In some locations, fuel is definitely scarce, so use small fires—or carry a primus stove. Fires should not be kindled near the roots of trees, dead wood, moss, or forest duff, but in some open space on rock or earth. When breaking camp, let your fire burn all garbage and fuel completely so as to leave the smallest possible fire scar, then be sure it is completely out. Be sure to clean your campsite. Never throw bottles, cans, jars, or refuse in streams or lakes.

5. Do not try to cover too much country in one day. Carry a light pack. Keep warm. Include in your pack a flashlight, water-proof matches, and a pocket first-aid kit. Your trip in the mountains should be a pleasant experience, not an ordeal.

6. Trails penetrate most areas in both Parks and are maintained for your benefit. Avoid short-cutting especially on switchbacks since this greatly accelerates the erosion along trails. Rock climbing is hazardous due to the composition of the formations. It is a good idea to stay on established trails.

7. If you are lost or injured do not panic, keep your head. Sit down, rest, think. If you are lost, try to figure out where you are. If it is close to dark, find a place to camp, gather firewood, keep warm, and rest. Three smokes, three fires, three shouts, or three of almost anything that will attract attention will start help on the way.

8. Picking flowers or collecting specimens of plants, animals, or other natural or historical objects is prohibited without written authorization obtained in advance from the Superintendent. (No permits are issued for personal collections.)

9. On the trails, saddle and pack stock have the right of way at all times. Hikers shall move off the trail and remain still until the stock passes. Guide will proceed slowly with stock party after the hikers are in a safe location off the trail. Horses should not be permitted to walk on the oil-surfaced roads except where designated trails cross such roads.

10. Motorcycles, other motor vehicles, or bicycles must not be operated on the trails. You must not operate a vehicle outside the roadways or designated parking areas. Dogs or cats are not permitted on any trail in either Park. (Not even on a leash.)

The foregoing regulations and suggestions have evolved through many years of Park management. Obviously, they are meant to protect both you as a back-country traveler and both Parks themselves so that your visits will be worth while. Know and abide by them to get the most enjoyment from your trail trips.

MOUNTAINEERING IN THE TETONS

Few visitors can view the ragged Teton range without at least wondering what it would feel like to stand on the summits of these majestic peaks. It is not at all difficult to understand why mountain climbing is one of the major activities among many of the people who come to the Park, and why climbers come from all over the world to climb in these mountains. Mountain climbing, in the true sense of the term, is not done in Yellowstone National Park because of the lack of challenging peaks.

Several thousand people have by now scaled the Grand Teton (13,766 feet), written their names in the register at its rocky summit, and become members of the special fellowship of those who have climbed such a mountain. Some of these are veteran mountaineers; others are novices who, after attending the intensive climbing school for a day, have been given permission, because of their aptitude, to join the next guided party scheduled to go up the Grand. (There are several routes, of varying degrees of difficulty.)

How to begin? The fastest and surest way to learn is by enrolling in the Park-approved Exum School of American Mountaineering, which has headquarters at Jenny Lake. The next fine day you will find yourself sitting under a tree near Hidden Falls being checked out on ropes, carabiners, and pitons. Your companions will be young and old from all parts of the United States, and some from other countries. About an hour later, a rope around your waist, you will shout to your climbing partner, who is *belaying* (securing) you, "CLIMBING!" And as soon as he shouts reassuringly, "CLIMB," you will begin to crawl up the slippery rock on all fours, like a spider, and your climbing days will have begun. At the end of the afternoon, you will be swinging off the top of a cliff in a 20-foot rappel, and after that you will never be entirely happy until you have climbed a major peak.

Some start by climbing lesser mountains for practice; others, given permission, prepare for the Grand, and one afternoon set out with a guided party for the overnight bivouac in the saddle of the mountain. Final ascent is made in the early hours of the next morning, with the return to the valley the evening of the same day. It is a strenuous, demanding climb, and one of the most popular offered anywhere in the United States.

Two-day trips are required also for Mounts Moran (12,594 feet) and Owen (12,922 feet). Most of the other peaks of the Park may be ascended and descended the same day although early starts are rather essential.

The mountain climbing season in Grand Teton National Park

usually extends from June 15 to September 15. Climbing in early June is somewhat hazardous because of snow and ice conditions and falling rocks. Climbing after the middle of September is subject to sudden severe storms and cold weather conditions. Winter climbing is only permitted by special arrangements with the Superintendent.

Climbing equipment must be furnished by the individual climber. Basic equipment items may be purchased in the town of Jackson. While equipment requirements vary with each climb, visiting climbers should bring one or two standard nylon climbing ropes, ice axe, crampons, assorted pitons, piton hammer, carabiners, sling ropes, and climbing boots. The rubber-lug-soled boot has proven very acceptable for climbing in the Tetons. Other items of equipment should include warm clothes, gloves, tent, sleeping bag, and the usual cooking and eating gear. Food may be purchased at stores in Jackson.

Mountain climbing guide service is available at the Exum School of American Mountaineering at Jenny Lake. Qualified guides may be secured for all Park climbs. Equipment is furnished by the concessioner *only* to those persons utilizing the guide service or climbing school.

MOUNTAIN CLIMBING REGULATIONS

The National Park Service's main desire is to promote good mountaineering and to prevent accidents. In pursuit of these aims, the following regulations have been established:

1. *Solo Climbing.* No person shall climb alone on rock, snow, or ice regardless of location. This also means that parties must not leave one member alone at any time while climbing. Quite frequently individual climbers meet at the ranger station and form parties for the various climbs. Many an enduring friendship among climbers has originated in this manner.

2. *Signing Out and In.* Each climber must register in person at the Jenny Lake Ranger Station, and all parties climbing on rock, snow, or ice must sign out in person prior to each climb. *All parties are required to sign in immediately upon return from climbs.* Information regarding climb should be entered on the back of Climbers Registration Card. If the ranger station is closed, individual climbing cards are to be left in box provided. Equipment must be displayed when signing out. Notes left at the Registration Office do *not* constitute a valid sign out.

3. *Permission to Climb.* Climbing may be undertaken only with the permission of the Superintendent who has delegated this

authority to qualified mountaineer rangers stationed at Jenny Lake. Rangers will grant or deny permission for each specific climb, after considering the climber's experience, equipment, and knowledge of routes. On occasions, where the qualifications of the climbers do not measure up to the requirements of the climb he has proposed, the rangers will recommend other less difficult climbs that serve as conditioners for the more difficult routes. Such suggestions and recommendations are welcomed by the climbers who invariably show profound respect for the judgment of the rangers. Actually, complete and accurate climbing information may be obtained from the registration rangers at the Jenny Lake Ranger Station. These men have current information concerning the nature and condition of the climbing routes, equipment requirements, distances involved, and time factors. Many photographs of the peaks and routes are available for your examination. These rangers are willing and able to assist you in planning any climb in the Park.

4. *Leadership*. The leader of any party is responsible for keeping the party within the above regulations. If no leader is designated, all members of the party assume this responsibility. No person shall be permitted to join parties that have already signed out unless prior arrangements have been made. Ascents of several peaks from one or more high base camps require considerable flexibility in planning. The major point to remember is that if there is a remote possibility that a mountain will be attempted, it must be registered for. The registration ranger, with the climbing leader, will help to make out a tentative day-by-day itinerary that includes rest days and relocations of the base camp. Inclement weather, sickness, and personality conflicts may alter the itinerary, but under all conditions it is the leader's responsibility to see that the party stays within the scope of peaks and routes signed out for. Any change in climbing schedule should be indicated by a note left in a conspicuous place at their base camp. Extended trips of more than five days are discouraged unless arrangements are made to send down word that all is well.

5. *Finally*. It is understood that the National Park Service assumes no responsibility for accidents in the mountains and that part, or all, of the expense of rescue may have to be covered by the climbing party involved. All injuries must be reported to the Ranger Station immediately.

Chapter 6.

Plantlife of the Parks

THE principal features of the Parks' flora which attract the attention of the visitor are the forests and flowers of the Teton-Yellowstone region. But vegetation is important both of itself, and as background or accent. Plant cover or a lack of it is a major element responsible for varying biotic communities which add so much to the Parks. People are greatly interested in the Parks' wildlife, which would not live without the habitat requirements of the individual species. Vegetation provides background and color contrast for the scenic wonders. To those whose special interest may be some form of botany, the vegetation itself is primary.

The vegetated portions of the Parks may be divided into seven types of communities:

1. *Aquatic Communities*. These are found in the streams and lakes, and are made up of plants that grow in flowing or standing water.

2. *Sagebrush-Grass Community*. This community is lower than 7,000 feet and found primarily in the Gardner, Yellowstone, Lamar, and Snake River valleys and in the Jackson Hole region.

3. *Alpine and Subalpine Meadows*. The alpine meadows are those that are above timberline while the subalpine meadows are those that are below timberline. (Timberline in the Parks is at approximately 10,000 feet elevation.) The chief difference in the appearance of the two is due to the fact that all alpine plants are dwarf. Both alpine and subalpine meadows display a riot of wildflower color throughout the summer season.

4. *Douglas-Fir Forest*. This is a climax type of forest (see page 122) in the Rocky Mountains, but in the Teton-Yellowstone region, it is very limited. It is best seen in the vicinity of Tower Fall.

5. *Lodgepole-Pine Forest*. This is the most extensive type of plant community in the Parks, mostly between 7,000 and 8,500 feet elevation.

6. *Aspen Forest*. Scattered groves of the most common broad-leaved trees in both Parks are situated where the moisture is suitable.

7. *Spruce-Fir Forest*. Engelmann spruce and alpine fir are the climax tree species in most of the two parks from timberline down to 7,500 feet or lower. A convenient place to see this type of forest at close range is along sections of the West Thumb—Lake Junction road.

FORESTS OF YELLOWSTONE AND GRAND TETON

The most prominent feature of the Parks' flora is their forest growth, which covers approximately 80 per cent of these areas. The trees are nearly all conifer (cone bearing trees with ever-green leaves), but the species are few in number. Probably over three-fourths of the forests consists of the lodgepole pine (*Pinus contorta*). It grows in tall, straight, slender trunks, with little foliage, except near the top. The trees stand so close together that lower limbs of earlier growths die out and the individual tree is often said to be a tall telephone pole of 60 to 75 feet, with a Christmas tree on the top. (Because of their rather superficial root systems, they are not very well anchored and the forest floor is usually littered with fallen trees.) The Indians used the slender trunks of smaller trees for the framework of their tepees or lodges, hence the common name Lodgepole. It is the only two-needled pine in the Parks, the needles growing in bundles of two and seldom over 2½ inches in length. The cones are small, 1 to 2 inches long, and some of the older trees will keep several hundred closed cones on the tree for a number of years. Although normally most pine cones mature and are shed in two years, many of these lodgepole cones persist on the tree, closed until exposed to con-siderable heat. Thus heat from a fire opens the cone scales allow-ing thousands of seeds to fall upon a soil from which the fire has most likely burned much of the organic matter. A mineral soil ex-posed to direct sunlight is particularly favorable for lodgepole pine seedlings and these trees are one of the first to re-populate burned areas. Under normal conditions it makes such dense shade, it cannot reproduce and ultimately gives way to spruce and fir—both shade-tolerant trees.

The limber pine (*Pinus flexilis*) is found in the lower altitudes in both Parks, but this five-needled pine is seldom found in pure

118

stands. The young branches of this tree may be bent double without breaking, thus giving rise to its name. Since the leaves cannot withstand the shade of the branches the tree is rather bare near the center. The tree is usually 40 to 50 feet high, with a short trunk 2 to 5 feet in diameter. The stout, long-persistent branches ultimately form a low, wide, round-topped head. It is not a very shapely tree, and is interesting rather from its sturdy form than from any real beauty or symmetry.

Closely resembling the limber pine is the whitebark pine (*Pinus albicaulis*) a related species of the higher altitudes. It dominates the summits of the lesser mountains of the Parks and places of similar elevation where it is just a low, shrubby pine struggling against all the odds of an exposed and bleak habitat. The tree is usually 15 to 30 feet high, rarely 40 feet, generally with a short trunk 2 to 4 feet in diameter topped by an irregular, broad head. (Two miles beyond the forks leading into South Cascade Canyon of Grand Teton Park, one of the world's largest whitebark pines grows within 150 feet of the trail.) The needles of this species are in bunches of five, similar to the limber pine, but the cones are purplish in color in contrast to the yellow-green ones of the limber species.

The alpine fir (*Abies lasiocarpa*) is easily recognized by the erect plump cones, which resemble Christmas candles, at the top of the tree. One will seldom be rewarded by finding the soft, dark purple cones beneath the tree, as the cones disintegrate on the tree and seeds drop to the ground. The thin, silvery-white bark of the young trees and the blue-green of the needles makes a contrast of color never to be forgotten. The bark of the older trees becomes thicker and is roughened by thick, closely appressed, cinnamon-red scales. The bark is covered with pitch blisters which are filled with rank-smelling, viscid balsam which Indians used as a healing medicine and antiseptic. The alpine fir is also a favorite winter food of the moose. They eat the green needles and twigs, often stripping the entire tree as high as they can reach and as low as they can paw down into the snow. Many of the firs in the Parks have been heavily browsed, and you can readily see the "high-line" at the maximum height a moose can reach. While at high elevations this fir is very small and stunted, it grows into a fairly large tree (75 to 80 feet) at the lower elevations. In some locations, the deep winter snows pile on the lower branches of the alpine fir pressing them against the ground. There they take root and form a circle of smaller trees around the base of the parent tree. Such a colony is called "a snowmat of alpine fir."

The Engelmann spruce (*Picea engelmannii*) is a tall, well-developed tree, with symmetrical branches—commencing but

119

slightly above the earth, and drooping slightly as if pressed down by the weight of many winters' snow. The bark is of a light reddish hue, which contrasts beautifully with the dark foliage. In contrast to the alpine fir, the needles are sharp and pointed, are distributed all around the branches, leave the branches much roughened when they fall, and the cones hang pendant from the upper third of the tree. The needles are also square in cross section as compared to the flattened needles of the fir. Engelmann spruce inhabits the canyons of the Teton range above 7,000 feet and, in Yellowstone, it grows in shaded, moist ravines in such places as Keppler Cascade, Apollinaris Spring, Spring Creek, and the South Entrance of the Park.

While the blue spruce (*Picea pungens*) seems to be completely missing in Yellowstone, it is fairly common along the Snake River as it winds its way through the Grand Teton Park. While similar to the Engelmann spruce, the blue species can be easily distinguished by the following: the seed cones of the blue spruce are nearly twice the length of Engelmann spruce, and the bark of the former has a light reddish hue and is divided into vertical ridges, while the latter lacks the ridges and is more scaly. The bluish to silvery-green appearance of the blue spruce is caused by a fine powdery substance on the surface of the needles. The needles, themselves, are stiff, four-angled in shape, and sharp to the touch.

The Douglas fir (*Pseudotsuga menziesii*) is found most abundantly in the northern portions of Yellowstone, but to a considerable extent also in various other sections of both Parks. In size of trunk it is by far the largest tree in the Parks, occasional specimens exceeding 6 feet in diameter, and it grows more rapidly than any other conifer. The long, pendulous, lateral branches and the bracted cones are the two most characteristic features of the Douglas fir. No other tree in the entire region has the scales of the cone subtended by a three-forked bract. The older trees and those in higher altitudes often do not bear cones.

The Parks have two species of juniper, the *Juniperus communis* (the common mountain juniper) and the *Juniperus scopulorum* (the Rocky Mountain juniper). The common juniper, with awl-shaped leaves, would hardly be called a tree by most persons, as it trails over the ground in the shade of the lodgepole pine and looks like a spreading shrub, sometimes reaching a height of 4 feet. The green berries scattered along the branches are a year old and the blue, glaucous berries so often seen are two years old. If the animal life of the Parks would leave them alone they would remain on the trees for a number of years. The Indians cooked and ate them, and the pioneer used them for medicine.

The Rocky Mountain Juniper is a small tree or shrub with

120

brown, fissured bark that can be seen at low elevations in the Parks. Its pale to dark green needles are scale-like and its fruit is berry-like, dark blue. Many experts claim that these small junipers are among the oldest living things of the area. Some of these gnarled and twisted, shreddy-barked veterans of the storms of the decades are over five hundred years of age, although much stunted in size and distorted in shape.

The deciduous, broadleaved trees (they lose their leaves in the winter) are represented in the Parks by few species. The narrow-leafed cottonwood (*Populus angustifolia*) grows along the streams in the lower altitudes, but is not very abundant within the Grand Teton-Yelowstone Park area. The black cottonwood (*Populus trichocarpa*) is the largest deciduous tree in the two Parks, but is rather an infrequent occurrence. While the angustifolia species has narrow, lance-shaped leaves, those of the black cottonwood are fairly large, broadly ovate and are often up to 5 inches in length.

The quaking aspen (*Populus tremuloides*) is the most common deciduous tree to be found in Grand Teton and Yellowstone Parks. It is found all over the region but most abundantly at the lower levels. The greenish-white bark and fresh, green, trembling leaves stand out in marked contrast to the dark somberness of the coniferous woods. In certain localities the tree grows to a height of 30 or 40 feet. But it has its problems. Its bark is one of the favorite foods of the beavers. They fell the trees and cut the larger ones into lengths that they can drag to their pond. In the winter they eat the inner bark and then float the poles out into the pond to help make the dam. When the pine nuts are gone the squirrels nibble the bark and buds. Mice often girdle the trees, and birds eat the buds in the spring when the supply of berries is exhausted. In times of famine the elk and deer eat the bark from the aspen trees. Most of the trees bear as black marks the scars resulting from the browsing of the deer and elk. The aspen's leaves are attacked both by the aspen-leaf blight and the engraver moth. (The latter creates the intricate patterns that are often seen on the leaves of this member of the willow family.) Bracket fungus also frequently penetrates their trunks. But in spite of all its diffi-culties, the quaking aspen is one of the most beautiful trees of the Parks.

The species just described include all the trees of the Teton-Yellowstone region. There are besides several smaller growths and numerous low shrubs that are scarcely to be considered as forming a part of the forest. Willow thickets abound on nearly all the streams, and in some places, as in Willow Park, and along the Snake River, are very beautiful either in early spring or late autumn. Alder growths abound on nearly all streams. The dwarf birch also frequents the shores of some of the streams in the canyons of the Tetons and south of Old Faithful near Firehole River bridge. The Douglas, or mountain, maple is quite common around Mammoth Hot Springs, and on the lower, eastern slopes of the Teton range, and is a very pretty drawf tree. But these and other small shrubs make up only a very small portion of the vegetation of the Parks.

In the Parks, the forest community is always changing—rocks are being transformed into soil; one kind of plant is being replaced by another; animal populations dependent on specific plants change as the vegetation changes. There are many plants which, like the pines, grow successfully for a time—but finally *change* the very ecological conditions they need to survive. There is a pattern to this change, as one group of plants after another exploits and develops a new environment, making it possbile for another group of species to invade.

After glaciers had scoured the mountains and valleys to bare rock and raw mineral soil, the first plants to grow in this new environment were encrusted lichens. Eons may pass before these tiny plants may be able even faintly to alter the bare rock environment—but gradually the rock surface is changed enough so that more advanced leafy lichens or even primitive mosses may grow. These plants change conditions faster, and in niches and cracks enough humus gathers for the light wind-blown seeds of annual forms to germinate. Each season their dying foliage builds up the soil until it is fertile enough for perennial plants, grasses, shrubs, and pines to grow. The lodgepoles and their understory of shrubs and perennials develop together. Finally spruce and fir replace the pine and the forest has a degree of permanence, for the spruce and fir *do* germinate and grow on humus soils in the shade of older trees—so that the spruce-fir forest is continuing until fire, man, or another climatic change disturbs this balance.

Although the forest of the region has many enemies, its worst one is that demon—fire. Forest fires in the Parks arise from two principal causes: lightning and man. The Park Service in Grand Teton Park, for example, estimates that lightning causes 38 per cent of forest fires; man's carelessness causes 62 per cent. Since there is no control over lightning, we must concentrate our efforts on man-caused fires. This will never be entirely eliminated until everyone who visits the Parks realizes his responsibility. When the careless camper learns to extinguish his campfire thoroughly, and the thoughtless smoker to put out his cigarette before he tosses it aside, the fire hazard will be greatly lessened. One moment of thoughtlessness may result in the devastation and denudation of

122

the beauty of America's much-beloved playgrounds. When everyone realizes the deepest meaning of that thought in back of the founding of the National Park System and embodied in the words of the Roosevelt Arch over the Northern Entrance to Yellowstone, then and only then will everyone derive the greatest pleasure from a visit. There is no place for the note of selfishness in the words, *"For the benefit and enjoyment of all the people."*

FOSSIL FORESTS OF YELLOWSTONE

Not all the forests of Yellowstone are composed of living trees. The largest fossil, or petrified, forests known to man are located in the Park.

Yellowstone country, as it was in ancient times fifty-five million years ago, has been described as a relatively flat plains area with an altitude of only 2,000 feet and a climate similar to Virginia and the Carolinas. Hardwood trees, including sycamores, oaks, maples, hickories, dogwoods, walnuts, and chestnuts, flourished in heavy stands larger than evergreens. Study of the numerous specimens in the fossil forest area has revealed a succession of forests composed of more than one hundred different species of plants, including ferns, rushes, conifers and flowering plants. Earthquakes rumbled across the forested valleys and frightened animals fled as a slumbering volcano exploded. Volcanic ash was spewed across two-thirds of the two-million acres of wilderness, now known as Yellowstone Park, and lava flows engulfed and killed much of the forest. Out of ground water, the buried trees absorbed dissolved silica from the mud and ash. When the minute tubular cells of the wood become filled with silica, the structure of the original wood, knots, and annual rings, is so well preserved that the species of each tree may be easily determined. The bright colors in the petrified wood are due to the various salts in the percolating water, chiefly iron. The petrified trees are so hard that erosion wore down the slopes faster than the giant fossils.

After one forest was buried by mud and lava during the volcanic activity, another forest took root on top of the debris. This process was repeated for about twenty to thirty thousand years in the Yellowstone area so that successive layers of ash, reaching depths of 2,000 feet, contain entire petrified forests. Twenty-seven layers of fossilized trees have been found along cliffs in the Lamar River district.

In many respects, the fossil forests of Yellowstone are the most remarkable of their kind anywhere in the world. Among their unusual features are:

1. They cover a larger area—more than 40 square miles—than any other fossil forests known.

2. The petrified trees are mostly still standing upright in the same positions and at the same sites in which they grew, millions of years ago. So-called fossil forests in other areas, such as Arizona, California, and Egypt, are scattered, petrified driftwood.

3. And, in addition to tree trunks, the volcanic rocks of the fossil forest have been the source of thousands of beautiful fossilized leaves, twigs, needles, cones, and seeds.

Exposures of fossilized wood have been found across almost the entire northern section of the Park, and into the Snowy Range and Gallatin Mountains in Montana. The most outstanding and extensive exposures of fossil trees in the Park occur on the south side of the Lamar River, along the north slopes of Amethyst Mountain and Specimen Ridge. In this section fossil trees are exposed over an area of about 20 square miles. Specimen Ridge contains some of the finest fossil trees in the Park, but this area is reached by foot trail only. Guided ranger-naturalist hikes, lasting six hours, are conducted two days a week from Lamar River Bridge (Northeast Entrance Road) to the fascinating petrified forests on Specimen Ridge. Be sure to bring a lunch, water, good hiking shoes, and a jacket.

To the east and northeast of the Fossil Forest, there are other fossil areas where petrified stumps have been found. On Calfee and Miller Creeks and on the south bank of Cache Creek, about 7 miles above its mouth, are important sites. In the same general region stumps are found on the slopes of The Thunderer and on Barronette, Bison, and Abiathar Peaks. About 5 miles west and north of Specimen Ridge is another important area of tree petrification. It is sometimes referred to as the "Petrified Tree Road," and is reached from the Grand Loop Highway, near Roosevelt Lodge. It is here that a large fossil tree is enclosed in an iron cage. In the early history of the Park the slopes in this area were dotted with fossil stumps, but "human erosion" became so effective in removal of fossil wood that the caged stump is now the only one standing out in relief in this area.

Some of the finest leaf impressions in the Park have been found on the slopes west of the caged tree, on the old Crescent Hill Road. Another area that is noted for fossil leaves, as well as petrified stumps and logs, lies almost directly north of Crescent Hill, on the north bank of the Yellowstone River. It can be reached only by trail, and is from one-half to 2 miles above the mouth of Hellroaring Creek.

There is an important area of tree fossilization in the Gallatin

124

Mountains in the northwestern corner of the Park. This area is very large and spreads into Tom Miner's Basin and into the Cedar Creek drainage in Montana. The most accessible exposures in the Gallatin Mountains in the Park are found in the steep bluffs north of Specimen Creek. This fossil area is located a little over a mile northeast of the Gallatin Ranger Station.

WILDFLOWERS OF THE PARKS

The wildflowers of Teton-Yellowstone regions are one of the major attractions of the Parks. They grow almost everywhere, and one rarely finds a spot so sterile (except around geysers and hot springs) that Nature has failed to beautify it with some simple blossom. It is impossible, within the limits of this chapter, to give a full description of the flowers of the two Parks, for they run well up into the hundreds. We can, however, note some of the more important species—those that you are almost sure to see on your tour, particularly if made in the latter part of June or early in July. A few species disappear early in the season, and many of them disappear before the first of August. However, because of the different elevations, a large proportion of the flowers can be seen in one location or another for nearly the entire season.

Even before the snow in the valley of the Parks recedes, the early sagebrush buttercup (*Ranunculus jovis*) pushes up through snowbanks to pit its warm golden hue against the cold white remnants of winter. It is soon followed by the pasqueflower, waterleaf, shootingstar, yellowbell, steershead, springbeauty, and the *Lomatiums*. These harbingers of spring are usually reserved only for the enjoyment of winter residents, and after the long winter with its deep snows, they are joyously welcomed.

The lungwort (*Boraginacene mertensia*) is another early arrival, and its large blue clusters grow in great numbers on the hills between Mammoth Hot Sprngs and the Golden Gate, but is seldom seen in the Tetons. Two other members of the family, mountain bluebell and alpine bluebell, however, are common in both Parks. The latter, which is deep blue in color and grows in thick clusters close to the ground, is found only at high altitudes, almost at the mountain summits, in fact. The mountain species, which has a tubular blue flower and its plant reaches a height of two or more feet, inhabits subalpine areas and can be found along trails like the one to Lake Solitude, or roads like the highway over Dunraven Pass. Another bluebell, the oblong-leaf species, is common in sagebrush areas.

125

Wildflowers delight the eye in Yellowstone-Grand Teton region.

A flower that can be observed almost everywhere in both Parks in the early spring, soon after the snow disappears, is the phlox (*Phlox,* in six species). It grows close to the ground in compact masses, which form mats of delicately tinted blossoms, ranging in color from white and pink to lavender. It is one of the very few wildflowers that has a real fragrance, and its odor fills the air wherever it grows.

The scarlet gilia (*Gilia aggregata*) is one of the most brilliantly colored and showy of the Grand Teton National Park's wildflowers. It is found also near the South Entrance of Yellowstone. A member of the phlox family, it produces only a small clump of

126

basal leaves the first year, followed by a 2-foot flowering stock the second year.

Violets (*Violas*) are found in seven or eight distinct species; but since their season is rather short and early in the season, they are not often seen by visitors of the Parks.

A flower present in a fascinating variety of species throughout both Parks is the Indian paintbrush (*Castilleja rhexifolia*), or Wyoming painted cup. It is a very common plant that appears in several species and its color shadings are from pale-cream through yellows and pinks to every shade of red imaginable. It is an interesting fact that the real blossom of this brilliant plant is so small to be scarcely perceptible. What gives it its wealth of color is the leaf which grows in thick clusters at the top of the stem to protect the tiny blossoms it conceals. The Indian paintbrush is the state flower of Wyoming.

Speaking of official flowers, Yellowstone National Park has one: the fringed gentian (*Gentiana thermalis*). Its deep rich blue color is found in no other flower, and there are few flowers which, on close inspection, display so fine a texture. It can usually be found blooming somewhere in the more moist open, subalpine sections of Yellowstone from June to September. However, in Grand Teton National Park it occurs in rather limited areas such as along the main highway a mile or so north of Jackson Lake Dam during August.

What is considered by many as the most beautiful flower in the Parks is the columbine (*Aquilegia coerulea*). Certainly, in grace of form and delicacy of coloring it is unsurpassed. The palest are cream-white, and others seem made up of every dainty shade of yellow, pink, blue, and purple. The plant grows about a foot high, with pendant blossom, swinging like a bell from its slender stem. It brightens up the canyon trails through open forests up to about 9,000 feet. The columbine is the state flower of Colorado.

Another attractive flower is the bright blue larkspur (*Delphinium,* in five species) which is found in almost every portion of both Parks.

Another member of the crowfoot plant family, the monkshood, flourishes best in the wet meadows and stream banks up to 9,000 feet in the major canyons. The flowers are generally purple but occasional white ones occur.

The sulphurflower or umbrellaplant (*Eriogonum,* seven or eight species) can be seen in large numbers through the mountain regions of both Parks—often covering the mountainsides with its varied shades of yellow, red, and cream white.

Actually one of the most abundant flowers in the Teton-Yellowstone region is the lupine (*Lupinus,* in more than ten species). It

127

grows almost everywhere, and is found in masses on the grassy mountainside in every shade of color—from a lavender so pale as to be almost white, to the deepest purple or blue.

Another profuse flower in certain areas of the Parks is the fireweed (*Epilobium angustifolium*). This plant gets its name from the fact that it grows in areas that have been devastated by fire. Its long clusters of magenta-pink flowers are set on stems from 1 to 5 feet in height. Its leaves take on a brilliant red in the fall. Fireweed decorates the hillside and roadways in all regions.

Another magenta-colored flower is the wild geranium (*Geranium viscosissimum*), which has conspicuous blossoms that are seen along the roadsides. Its leaves also turn red in the autumn.

Clinging to the rocks around Yellowstone's Golden Gate and open sunny slopes in the Tetons may be seen the evening primrose or moonrose (*Oenothera,* four species). Its large beautiful blossoms open at sunset and close about noon. They are white at first, but gradually turn a deep rose-pink. A yellow evening primrose is very common along roadsides in Jackson Hole.

No flower is more interesting than the monkey flower or false snapdragon. The first ones to appear around Old Faithful are about 1½ inches tall, bearing deep reddish-purple flowers. They carpet the slopes below the Inn. Later a yellow one blooms in the hot run-off streams from the geysers and hot springs, growing in water many degrees warmer than you would care to keep your hand in. Then a larger yellow monkey flower forms yellow beds about all of the warm springs of the region, and one can almost trace the course of the lukewarm streams by the yellow blossoms. Later a deep-red monkey flower, whose flowers are about 1½ inches long, blooms along the cold streams of Yellowstone. The red snapdragon and wild geranium bloom profusely along the road from Old Faithful to West Thumb and on part of the slopes of Mount Washburn. The monkey flower is very common in Jackson Valley, too. If you have a vivid enough imagination you will probably see the grinning face of an ape in the face of the flower, and it is from this peculiarity that it gets its name, *Mimulus*.

The yellow water lily (*Nymphaea polysepala*) is found in great abundance in some of the lakes and ponds in Yellowstone. It is particularly noticeable in Isa Lake at the first crossing of the Continental Divide above the Upper Geyser Basin.

The harebell (*Campanula rotundifola*), or bluebell of Scotland, is a common flower in the Parks. Its flowers are purplish-blue, nodding and bell-like. It grows in clusters along the roadside, on open slopes, and hillsides.

The aster (members of the composite family) is one of the first flowers of spring and the last to disappear in the fall. It is found

128

in not fewer than twelve distinct species throughout both Parks. Blossoms of purple, lavender, and blue are most common.

A brilliant flower, though more rarely seen by visitors, is the blue-pentstemon, or beardtongue (*Pentstemon*), and there are no fewer than sixteen species of this genus in both Parks. These various species grow from the valley floor to high alpine areas.

The sunflower (*Helianthus*) is represented by several species and grows in great profusion in Yellowstone, but is found in only a few localities in Grand Teton Park. There also are many genera of fleabane in the Parks and they range in colors from white and pink to purple and lavender. At lower elevations, balsamroot (arrowleaf) has large, yellow daisy-like flowers and large, arrow-shaped leaves.

In addition to the flowers just briefly described, the following may fall under the eye of the visitors: The anemone or windflower (*Anemone* in two species), a small white flower found at all elevations; the arnica plant (*Arnica,* seven species), a bright yellow flower growing in the shade of evergreen trees; the globemallow (*Sphaeralcea rivularis*), a large pink hollyhock-type flower; butter-and-eggs (*Linaria vulgaris*), yellow flowers resembling cultivated snapdragon; the elephant head (*Pedicularis groenlandica*) a purple spike that has an amazing resemblance to an elephant's head; the prickly-pear cactus (*Opuntia fragilis*), yellow flowers that can be found in dry locations; and the goldenrod (*Solidago,* in five species). The orchid family has numerous representatives in the Parks, the most important being the calypso orchid (*Calypso bulbosa*) and coralroot orchid (*Corallorrhiza maculata*).

Among the flowering shrubs and vines, the more prominent are: The wild rose, which is present in great abundance in the lower elevations and is conspicuous both for its beautiful blossoms in spring and its scarcely less beautiful foliage in fall; the spirea; the shadbush, or service-berry, which is covered with white flowers; the mountain ash; red-osier dogwood, with its foral clusters in the spring and white berries in the fall; Western Labrador tea; grouse whortleberry, which has nodding flowers of white to pink and juicy red fruits; rabbitbrush; honeysuckle (*Lonicera,* several species); chokecherry; hawthorn; bitterbrush; Oregon grape; and several varieties of berry bushes, and strawberry plants which grow all over both Parks. Poison ivy is rare—along the Gardner River north of Mammoth and small patches on the east and west shores of Jackson Lake. There is no poison oak in the Parks. However, the beautiful but destructive parasite, the mistletoe, is found on the lodgepole pine.

While there are several species of sagebrush in the Parks, the *Artemisia tridentata* is the most common and grows 2 or 3 feet high. (There are some exceptionally large bushes, nearly 10 feet in height, around Mammoth.) This dusty-gray bush of the Western plains has a three-prong leaf and is the state flower of Nevada.

There are several representatives of the fern family in the Parks, the most important being the brittlefern, or bladderfern (*Cystopteris fragilis*), which has a general distribution throughout the Teton-Yellowstone region. Also several of the grasses are exceedingly beautiful in their season of blossom, and, like the autumn leaves, deserve to be considered with the flowers.

YELLOWSTONE'S ALGAE

In Chapter 2, Yellowstone's famous algae that add beautiful colorings around hot springs and geysers were fully described. But there is another phase of the blue-green and the green algae that will be found interesting to the Parks' visitor. These are the previously mentioned lichens, which are formed by the association of certain algae and fungi, dual organisms. This association of two entirely different groups of the plant kingdom is known as symbiosis, and differs from parasitism, in which one of the plants derives the benefit at the expense of the other, in that symbiosis is where both plants profit, a sort of mutually beneficial arrangement. A fungus is a plant that is dependent upon organic material for its food. It has no green coloring material, chlorophyll, and therefore it cannot manufacture its own food. The algae are independent in this respect; given sunlight they can manufacture their food through the agent, chlorophyll, by a process known as photosynthesis (put together by light). In the lichen the fungus fastens itself to a rock or a tree where it could not obtain its own living. It thus becomes a home for the algae, being a means of support which holds the algae up in the sunlight. The fungus in the dual result, takes the food the algae produces, and the fungus keeps the upper hand in this partnership by not allowing the algae to multiply except within certain limits. While present in both Parks, we find a fine example of lichen growth in Yellowstone at the Golden Gate where the gold coloring of the rocks is due to a covering of them. Lichens are often beautiful, and their color range is broad. They are often brilliant reds, warm browns, blacks, grays, pea-greens and other more unusual colors in Nature. Thus, whether you climb to the highest peak, or walk through the deep woods, or over the hot spring terraces, you will find some plantlife growing in Yellowstone-Grand Teton Park area.

With a few exceptions, the flowers of the Parks are not particularly fragrant, and wilt fairly quickly should they be picked. Remember—DO NOT PICK WILDFLOWERS.

130

Chapter 7.

Wildlife of the Parks

YELLOWSTONE and Grand Teton National Parks, the largest wildlife sanctuaries in the United States, present a superb spectacle of native wild animals on a vast stage comprising more than 2½ million acres. Featuring the larger animals including moose, bighorn sheep, pronghorn or antelope, bison or buffalo, elk, mule deer, and bears, with an occasional coyote or mountain lion, this pageant of wild creatures affords the Park visitor unrivaled opportunities to observe and gain knowledge of the various species under a close approach to primitive conditions.

Leisurely travel, some understanding of animal habits, and binoculars, all aid in seeing wildlife. But remember that wildlife is constantly moving about. Some movements are seasonal and some governed by the time of day. Other factors, such as weather or food, may dictate where animals may be found. But, in general, if you are truly interested in seeing the Park wildlife, rise with the sun and ride or hike in the early morning through the forests and meadows. By 8 or 9 a.m., most of the mammals will have gone into seclusion, not to be seen again until evening when they come out into the open areas to feed. For photography, the morning hours are best. As far as seasons go, May, early June, late September, and October are the best months to observe wildlife in the Parks.

Of course, you cannot expect to see all the species reported to live in a region. Parks are not zoos and the animals are not kept in enclosures for the public to view. Some of the species are extremely secretive and shy; others are rare. But remember that the Parks are sanctuaries for wildlife, and feeding, hunting, killing, wounding, frightening, or capturing of any bird or other animal is prohibited. The use or display of firearms is also prohibited—possession of them must be declared at entrance station.

In all National Parks, the policy of maintaining an area as a wilderness zone just as it would operate naturally, with as little artificial interference as possible, is the goal to be achieved. Thus the Park Service limits road building and all types of construction to a minimum, allowing just enough artificial disturbance, so that you may enter the area and see the way Nature is caring for its own and has been doing so for hundreds of years. In all nature there is what is called a biotic balance; a balance between different species of animals, and between animals and plant life within an area. Briefly, as an example, it might be said that although many deer are killed each year by predators such as coyotes or cougars, the Park Service does not try to eliminate the predator, or interfere in any way in its pursuit of food and shelter, realizing that if they were to eliminate all predators of one species such as deer, the deer would increase in abundance above all capacity of the range to support them. And the deer as a result of being preserved from predators, would become weak, dying of disease and starvation.

As a whole the Park Service interferes very little with the normal lives of the animals within the Parks. You may help them to keep the biotic balance by not feeding the bears, because when bears expect handouts from humans and depend on such for their food, they gradually become dangerous and pestiferous, as well as less healthy, and rangers sometimes have to trap such bears, removing them from the area, or sometimes disposing of them by shooting. Generally speaking, all wild animals will be much more healthy if they are left to forage for themselves rather than depending on man for their proper nutritive balance. Fires also upset the biotic balance and destroy homes for wildlife, as well as animals themselves. Therefore, be careful with smokes, matches, and campfires while in the Parks.

The most difficult enemy in the Parks for an animal to cope with is the automobile. A great many of the squirrels are destroyed by speeding cars and some of the larger animals are not immune, especially at night when the glare from the headlights of an approaching car seems to blind the animals and cause them to leap in front of the automobile.

MAMMALS

There are over sixty species of mammals that occur (or did occur) in Grand Teton and Yellowstone Parks. The following short descriptions, plus the use of the checklist with standard animal field guides (see page 202), should aid you to identify species you may see. The text suggests likely locations where you may find the more common mammals.

For children, Yellowstone's best attraction are the bear cubs.

THE BEAR FAMILY

Two species of bears, the grizzly (*Horribilis*) and the black (*Euarctos americanus*), are found in both of the Parks, but the latter is by far the more numerous. Many people put the brown and cinnamon bear in a separate class, but they are all members of the black bear family—"blondes and brunettes," so to speak.

The black bear is a glossy smooth-coated animal with a tan or brown muzzle; short black curved claws, incapable of being withdrawn without tearing; small, erect, and almost-hidden ears; and a short and practically non-existent tail. They ordinarily stand 25 inches at the shoulders and above 5 feet from tip to tip. The grizzly is larger (standing about 3 to 3½ feet), with a pronounced hump at the shoulders; very long front claws; and a prominent forehead. They vary in color from a light yellow to almost black, with tips of their hairs having a grayish tinge. At maturity the black bear weighs from 300 to 400 pounds; grizzlies from 500 to 600 pounds. This is quite a size when you consider that a black bear cub, when born, during the winter sleep of the female, weighs only 8 to 12 ounces; a grizzly cub is around a pound when born. The cubs stay with their mothers for two summers.

There is quite a distinction between the walks of the two species. The grizzly has a shuffling walk that carries an indication of great power, whereas the black bear moves in a rather clumsy, awkward fashion. Nevertheless bears of either species will outrun an average horse and will often travel 40 or 50 miles in a day. Another big difference between species is that blacks climb trees while grizzlies do not. Grizzly cubs, before their claws begin to straighten, can scamper up a tree, but a mature grizzly cannot climb. All bears have very poor eyesight, but this is offset by their keen sense of hearing and smell.

Black bears are common throughout both Parks, though most frequently seen in the vicinity of campgrounds and picnic areas. In Yellowstone, they can be seen along most of the Park's roads, while in the Tetons black bears are seen occasionally along the lower mountain trails. Extreme care should be used in parking to watch bears so that you do not create a highway traffic hazard which endangers the lives of others. Do not encourage them to approach you and keep car windows closed when near bears. *Remember Park regulations prohibit feeding or molesting the bears.*

Many visitors to the Parks, upon observing the activities of the area's "hold-up" bears, fail to realize that the bear is a *wild* animal, and will not hesitate, in the least, to rip your arm or chest open with its curved claws, inflicting painful and costly injuries, if you try to fool it about food. Sometimes the bear thinks your camera

134

is food, so be careful when you attempt to photograph a bear. Then, too, remember that a mother bear usually never leaves her cubs very far away, even during the second summer, and will attack anyone she thinks is trying to molest them. If you happen to meet a bear on the trail, pay attention to your own business and the bear will usually try to get out of your way.

Bears that become too much of a nuisance around areas of human habitation are trapped in special bear traps and transported to remote sections of the Parks. Sometimes the same bear will return to the location where it was trapped 30 or 40 miles away and continue to be a pest, and the rangers trap it again. This may happen several times, and finally the rangers may have to shoot the bear if it causes too much damage. You can help the rangers to keep down the number of bears they have to dispose of by respecting park regulations, and thus not attracting bears to areas of artificial feeding. The natural food of bears varies considerably including berries, tender plant shoots, lily bulbs, as well as several types of animal life, including ground squirrels, grubs, ants, and other insect life.

You are not likely to see a grizzly bear along the main roads, but if you do, give him a wide berth. They are fairly common throughout Yellowstone, but in midsummer they often may be seen on the far side of the Yellowstone River in Hayden Valley and along back roads such as the old ones to Tower and Bunsen Peaks. In the spring they can be noted grazing in places such as the Gibbon Meadows and near Fishing Bridge.

ELK (*Cervus canadensis*)

If "Yellowstone is bear country," then Teton country is ruled by the wapiti (elk). These "monarchs of the Tetons" are large deer-like animals with a yellowish rump-patch and a small white tail. The body is reddish-brown in summer and brownish-gray in winter. The neck is usually dark brown in color, and males have a definite neck mane. The bull elk has heavy spreading antlers that are shed in late winter or early spring. During spring and summer new antlers are grown. Antlers vary in size from a single spike 1 foot long, for a very young bull, to 5 feet long with 6 tines or points on each beam, and a spread of over 5 feet.

During the first half of May in Teton Park, large groups of elk move across Antelope Flats, east of Jackson Hole Highway, in their annual return to their summering grounds. For the next month the cows are more solitary, seeking heavy cover for bearing their calves. Favorite calving areas in Teton are Burnt Ridge, Signal Mountain and vicinity, and a few other similar places. The

135

older bulls, for the most part, usually move on north into Yellowstone or to the higher elevations of the Teton Range. In July and August elk frequent the area between Signal Mountain and Burnt Ridge. If one drives along one of the gravel roads in this area and quietly parks his car, elk can be seen either about sunup or about sundown, moving out of the forest onto the open flats. Fall is the season when the mature bulls round up their harems of cows. At this time of year the elk are most easily observed and most exciting to watch. The area about Signal Mountain and Burnt Ridge is still the best part of the park to watch their activity and to hear the challenging bugle of the bulls. In early winter, the time depending on snow and weather, large bands of elk again will move across the open flats to their wintering area south of Grand Teton Park. A small herd of elk can also be found at the Jackson Hole Wildlife Range.

In Yellowstone National Park, elk can usually be seen in spring and fall in the meadows along the Madison River, the small meadows between Mammoth and Old Faithful, between Norris and Canyon, and from Yellowstone Lake to the East Entrance. The elk migrate to the higher meadows during the summer, but some remain in the meadows in the Norris region and the Clearwater Springs-Roaring Mountain area.

DEER

Mule deer (*Odocoileus hemionus*) is the only species of deer now inhabiting the two Parks. Formerly, a few whitetail deer (*Odocoileus virginianus*) were here in the lowland shrub areas, but this animal was unable to hold its own in competition for browse with large numbers of elk and other members of the deer family in the Parks. The mule species is a rather large deer with large ears and a good-sized patch of white on the rump and throat. The tip of the tail is black. While the summer color of the coat is tawny to yellowish brown, the winter coloration is rather dark gray.

In the summertime, mule deer are well scattered over Yellowstone, but the best spots to see them are in the Mammoth Hot Spring area (below the terraces and at Indian Creek), the road from Mammoth to Golden Gate, Swan Lake Flat, near Chittenden Bridge, and in three directions from West Thumb.

In Grand Teton Park they are most often seen by the visitor who hikes the trails. In summer the deer prefer the lower mountain slopes. In spring and fall they are moving between the mountain slopes and their wintering grounds, mostly south of Jackson. Because of deep snows, few deer winter in the Park.

136

Elk.

Yellowstone Park Company Photo.

Mule deer.

Yellowstone National Park Photo.

Pronghorns near Mammoth Hot Springs.
Yellowstone Park Company Photo.

MOOSE (*Alces alces*)

The moose is the largest of North American deer. The large, ungainly and grotesque-appearing moose is very unlike the graceful deer. It has an ugly face with a long nose, high and heavy shoulders, much smaller hindquarters than the deer, and long legs. These features make it seem a caricature. But in spite of the size, appearance, and mighty spread of antlers, the bull moose can, if he chooses, drift through the woodland as quiet as a mouse; then again he may give the sound effect of a herd of elephants on a stampede.

In Yellowstone, moose are most likely to be seen in Swan Lake Flat and Willow Park between Mammoth and Norris; along Northeast Entrance road; in the Dunraven Pass area; along Lewis River above Lewis Canyon, and between Fishing Bridge and the East Entrance. They are also numerous in the Falls River Basin, Pelican Creek (lower), Slough Creek areas, Lava Creek, Tower Junction area, and along the Yellowstone River above the Lake (Hayden Valley area).

In spring their favorite locations in Teton Park are Blacktail Ponds, northwest of Blacktail Butte; the Sawmill Ponds, along the Wilson Road; Moose Ponds, just south of Jenny Lake; and the Oxbow Bend, west of the Wildlife Range. Many browse in the Willow Flats near Jackson Lake Lodge. During summer, moose move into the spruce and cottonwood forests along the river bottoms. These may be seen by scanning the river bottoms from the scenic overlooks along the Jackson Hole Highway. In fall and winter the moose move into open country where they are easily observed. It is well to remember that moose are animals of uncertain temperament. One should be especially cautious of cows with calves.

PRONGHORN (*Antilocapra americana*)

The pronghorn, or American antelope, is one of the fastest-running animals in the world. It moves over the ground with great, bounding leaps. The pronghorn is the only creature in the world with horns that are branched, and each horn is curved and has a single prong. (Female's horns are only about 5 inches long; the buck's may be as long as 12 inches.) Every year, it sheds the outer cover of these—no other animal with horns does this. The basic coloration of this animal is reddish-brown or tan with darker brown to blackish mane and muzzle, white rump and whitish, or creamy, underparts.

In Grand Teton National Park, pronghorn occur in small bands

138

Yellowstone National Park Photo.

Bighorn sheep feeding near the North Entrance to Yellowstone.

Bull bison seen along Fountain Freight Road, Yellowstone.

Yellowstone National Park Photo.

on Antelope Flats, north of Kelly, during the summer months. They do not winter in the Park, however. In Yellowstone, they often may be observed along the old road between Mammoth and Gardiner; on the Blacktail Deer Plateau between Mammoth and Tower Junction; in Lamar Valley; and along the road from North Entrance to Reese Creek.

BISON (*Bison bison*)

The bison, or American buffalo, is the largest North American land mammal. Mature bulls weigh about 2,000 pounds, but cows are much smaller and weigh about half as much. Bulls and cows are both horned and have high-humped shoulders and short tails. The blackish-brown hair on the shoulders, neck, and head is long and woolly, while that on the hindquarters is dark brown and short in warm weather, but grows longer in cold weather.

During the fall, winter, and spring months, Yellowstone's bison can be found in Lamar Valley, Firehole Geyser Basin (especially around Firehole Lake), along the Fountain Freight road, and on Soda Butte. When warm weather arrives in June they begin to move to higher elevations, but a few wander, or remain, in the Lower Geyser Basin meadows, near Madison Junction, in Hayden and Lamar Valleys, and near Mary Bay, East Entrance road.

The bison is the only animal held in captivity in Grand Teton National Park. A small herd is in an enclosure known as the Jackson Hole Wildlife Range, a pasture just east of Oxbow Bend. At times they move back among the trees, where they are less obvious. So you must look for them carefully, but remember that even these bison are wild and must be treated with respect.

BIGHORN SHEEP (*Ovis canadensis*)

This species of sheep has big, curling horns that measure at the base from 15 to 18 inches for a mature ram. (Females have slender, short, and slightly curved horns.) They are gray-tan in color and have a large yellowish-white rump patch. The underparts are light colored. It is interesting to note that wild sheep have hair, not wool, as the name might imply.

During the summer in Yellowstone, they may be observed near the summit of Mounts Washburn and Everts, Specimen Ridge, and from the Fossil Forest trail. In the winter sheep may be seen on the slopes of Mount Everts above the road to Gardiner from Mammoth, and along the base of Soda Butte and Junction Butte. In Teton, bighorn are often seen in summer near the trail over Mount Hunt Divide, between Open and Granite Canyons.

140

THE DOG FAMILY

Chief among the doglike canines in the Parks is the coyote (*Canis latrans*). Its fur is thick, coarse, and in general, a grayish-brown in color; it is about the size of a small German shepherd dog. They are found everywhere in the Parks, and they are becoming as bold as black bear. But the best places to see coyotes are in the meadow and grassland regions of the Parks—the floor of Jackson Hole, in Hayden and Lamar Valleys, and near Mammoth.

The coyote's blood brother, the gray, or timber, wolf (*Canis lupus*), is no longer found in the Parks. The red fox (*Vulpes fulva*) is also seldom seen. In Yellowstone, they have been seen on rare occasions in Blacktail Valley, along the road from Tower to Mammoth.

THE CAT FAMILY

There are three members of the cat family in the Parks: Bobcat (*Lynx rufus*), lynx (*Lynx canadensis*), and mountain lion (*Felis concolor*). The bobcat and the lynx are greatly similar, yet have definite differences. Both animals are catlike in general appearance, but proportionately have longer, stouter legs and larger feet than a housecat. These animals weigh about 20 pounds —the lynx is somewhat larger than the bobcat. The fur of lynx is a grayish color, while the fur of the bobcat ranges from pale-brown to reddish-brown. The bobcat has shorter tufts on its ear tips than does the lynx, and the bobcat's tail tip is striped black on top and pale underneath. The tail of the lynx has black rings on it and is tipped with a single black cap. Both these animals are rare in the Teton-Yellowstone region.

The mountain lion, also known as the cougar, ranks as the world's fourth largest cat. The body of the male mountain lion— which is a tawny or dull yellowish-brown color—may be from 4 to 5½ feet long, and its tail from 2 to 3 feet more. The female is considerably smaller. A mature lion might weigh as much as 200 pounds but will average closer to the 130 to 150 pound range. While the cougar is rare today, they have been reported in the Tower area, Hayden Valley, and in the Mammoth-Sepulcher-Electric Peak area.

THE WEASEL FAMILY

Members of the weasel family are characterized by having a set of scent glands located at the base of the tail. The odors emitted vary from the almost pleasant musky scent of the marten to the repugnant scent of the mink and skunk. When alarmed these animals can eject the secretion of these glands, and with the aid of the swishing tail the droplets can be thrown considerable distances. The skunk is probably the best known and most notorious representative of the group. Striped skunks (*Mephitis mephitis*) are found in the Parks only in the cottonwood regions at the lower elevations.

The long-tailed weasel (*Mustela frenata*), the short-tailed weasel or ermine (*Mustela erminea*), and mink (*Mustela vison*) are similar in appearance and habits. All have a rather long, slim body with short, thick, soft fur. The feet are large with curved claws and the legs are short and stout. The head is placed low, narrowing abruptly to the muzzle, and the tail is well-furred. The long-tailed weasel—about 18 inches long in length—is colored golden to dark brown on its back and sides. The tip of the tail is black and the underside of the body is yellow-orange. The smaller short-tailed weasel—about 12 inches long—has chocolate-brown sides and back, while the underside is white or pale-yellow and the tail has a black tip. In the winter both species of weasels may turn entirely white, except for the black tip on the tail. The all-year-round coat of the mink, which is about 24 inches in length, is a rich, dark reddish or chocolate-brown color; the underside is slightly paler than the back of the animal.

The marten (*Martes americana*) and the fisher (*Martes pennanti*), are both members of the weasel family, and are alike in many respects. In proportion they resemble a large squirrel with a fox-like head. Martens weigh up to 2½ pounds; fishers up to 10 pounds. The length of the animals varies from an average of 2 feet for the marten to 3½ feet for the fisher; the tail constitutes about one third that length. The marten is colored a rich, golden-brown over most of its body; the tail, feet, and muzzle are slightly darker while the throat has an orange patch on it. The fisher is colored an ashy, brownish-gray with an overwash of black. The marten is fairly common throughout the wooded sections of both Parks; the fisher has only been reported in Yellowstone Park.

The badger (*Taxidea taxus*) is a large, powerful, flat-bodied member of the weasel family. The squat body, short legs and grizzled-gray color in conjunction with the white face markings will distinguish the badger from any other mammal in the Parks. They are often seen in the sagebrush valleys, especially in the northern part of Yellowstone, from Mammoth to Tower Junction, and in the Lamar Valley.

The river otter (*Lutra canadensis*) is one of the largest members of the weasel family, adults weighing up to 25 pounds. The body is long, and rather plump; the feet are large and webbed for swimming. The short, thick, soft fur is colored rich, dark chocolate-brown, fading to a lighter shade on the underside of the animal. The otter can be found along the Yellowstone River in Hayden Valley, shore of Yellowstone Lake, the Snake, Gibbon and other rivers in the Teton-Yellowstone region. The wolverine (*Gulo luscus*), another member of the weasel family, has seemingly left the Parks altogether.

THE RABBIT FAMILY

There are three species of rabbits found in the Parks: White-tail jackrabbit (*Lepus townsendii*), snowshoe hare (*Lepus americanus*) and cottontail rabbit (*Sylvilagus nuttallii*). The latter is found in only the low areas near the North Entrance of Yellowstone Park. While the other two species are fairly similar, their habitat serves best to distinguish them. Jackrabbits are found in the sagebrush and grasslands region, while the snowshoe hares frequent the conifer forests of the Parks.

THE RODENT FAMILY

Rodents are many and varied in the Parks, with adaptations for all types of habitat to be found among them. The porcupine (*Erethizan dorsatum*), a clumsy, quill-bearing bark-eater, is a menace to the night wanderer who is hardy enough to venture out without a flashlight. Half the life of the quill pig is spent in the treetops and the other half spent in search of a sweat-soaked shovel handle or greasy board, in fact any article with a suggestion of salt about it will have an irresistible attraction for him.

Beaver (*Castor canadensis*) and muskrat (*Ondatra zibethicus*), both well adapted to the aquatic life, are quite common in both Parks. The beaver, personification of industry, may occasionally be seen at work on one of its numerous work projects in such locations as the lower Shoshone Creek, small ponds in the Mammoth area, and Grayling Creek on the Gallatin side. In Teton, their projects are numerous in the Snake River watershed. Along the smaller tributary streams such as those that feed the Snake in Jackson Hole area, beaver build dams to conserve water for their protection, dig canals leading to their timber-cutting operations, and construct large, durable houses. Their value as a soil conservationist and flood-control agent is beginning to be truly appreciated. In appearance the beaver is not particularly handsome or graceful until seen in the water, where it is in its own element. Diving with tremendous splashes of its broad, scaly tail, or cruising along on the surface of the water, it has things well under control and is able to hold its own with most animals who invade its domain with a predatory objective in mind. The beaver has most of the fruits of his labors presented to the passing visitor in a most accessible fashion. The animal, itself, however, is mostly nocturnal and rarely seen except in the evening.

The muskrat follows the lead of the beaver in many of its activities except dam-building and tree-cutting. While mostly nocturnal, the muskrat is occasionally seen silently swimming along the surface of a pond or stream, or diving into the entrance of its nest in a cloud of muddy water. It is probable that much of the work of the muskrat is mistaken for beaver work, for they are often found living in close association. In appearance the muskrat resembles a common wharf rat except its fur is much denser and finer and its feet are webbed. The tail is flattened vertically, and the muskrat is more at home in the water than on land.

The chipmunks and the ground squirrels are almost everywhere in the Parks. There are three species of chipmunks—least, yellow-pine, and uinta—that exist here, but they are too much alike to be differentiated by the casual observer. Thus just call them all "chipmunks." But the golden-mantled ground squirrel, which has almost the same general appearance as a chipmunk, can be easily distinguished: the little chipmunk has four stripes along its back and down over its head and its face; the slightly larger golden-mantled ground squirrel has stripes running up each side only as far as its shoulder. The only other ground squirrel in the Parks —the uinta—is dull gray-brown without striping.

Red squirrels (*Tamiasciurus hudsonicus*) and Northern flying squirrels (*Glaucomys sabrinus*) are the only tree squirrels in the two-park area, but the latter, being nocturnal, is rarely, if ever, seen by visitors. (While this squirrel cannot fly in the true sense of the word, it is a marvelous glider and can sail with ease for a distance of 40 yards or more. It generally springs from the top of a tall tree and glides downward, checking its speed abruptly as it approaches the trunk of the tree on which it lands. The flattened tail serves as a rudder, and it can make surprisingly sharp turns in the course of its "flight.") The red squirrel is one of the common forest dwellers of the Parks. A reddish coat and light underparts make it one of the more attractive creatures of the woods. Its food is obtained from the cones of the various evergreens, and its cafeterias are marked by piles of cone scales discarded in the process of obtaining the seeds.

Alpine rockslides and meadows also yield several forms of rodent life. The most conspicuous is the yellowbelly marmot (*Marmota flaviventris*). This animal, which looks like a large,

144

ungainly ground squirrel with a short tail, is ochraceous color above and reddish below with golden-buff mantle on the anterior back. Another dweller in the high country, the pika or cony (*Ochotona princeps*) is a small, short-eared, member of the rabbit family with an un-rabbit-like habit of bleating. (The marmot makes his presence known by a piercing whistle; the pika, by a series of staccato squeaks that sound like a diminutive bark.) The name "alpine haymaker," which is sometimes used, refers to the pika's habit of gathering grasses and other plants that he stores for food as cured "hay."

The only true gopher in the Parks is the northern pocket gopher (*Thomomys talpoides*). The uinta ground squirrel is frequently referred to by some people as a gopher, but it should not be confused with the true gopher and is seldom seen above the ground. The pocket gopher is rather small in size, about 8 inches long, including a tail of a little over 2 inches, and is light brown in color.

Mice and voles are the most abundant animals in the Parks. The two, however, are easily distinguished. The nocturnal mice have large eyes and ears; voles have tiny eyes and small ears. The most numerous species of mice are: the deer mouse (widely distributed throughout the forested areas of the Parks at all elevations) bushytail woodrat or packrat (inhabits cracks or crevices in rocky cliffs from the valley floor to the timberline), and the Western jumping mouse (commonly found in wet meadows and along stream-banks at all elevations). Being nocturnal, mice are seldom seen by visitors to the Teton-Yellowstone area.

The voles and vole-like mammals are many—and difficult to identify. The most common species are: the Richardson vole (meadow mouse), mountain phenacomys (leming mouse), Boreal redback vole, meadow vole, mountain vole, longtail vole, and sagebrush vole.

THE SHREWS

Shrews are among the most primitive mammals that can be observed in the Parks. While they resemble mice—small, with grayish fur, long tails, and short feet—they are totally different and are completely unrelated. In contrast to mice, all shrews have long pointed snouts, pinpoint eyes, and almost invisible ears. The most common species found in the Parks are: the masked shrew (commonly found in forest regions at all elevations), the vagrant

(*Continued on page 147*)

CHECKLIST OF MAMMALS FOUND IN GRAND TETON AND YELLOWSTONE NATIONAL PARKS

KEY: #Relative abundance in favorable habitats: A—Abundant; C—Common; U—Uncommon; R—Rare; *—Known to have occurred in the Parks (presently absent or of unknown status; and †—captive herd.
T—Abundance in Grand Teton National Park
Y—Abundance in Yellowstone National Park
t—Recorded only from Grand Teton National Park
y—Recorded only from Yellowstone National Park

Abundance#	Name	Abundance#	Name
C	Black Bear	C	Yellowpine Chipmunk
CY-RT	Grizzly Bear	U	Uinta Chipmunk
A	Elk	C	Golden-mantled Ground Squirrel
C	Mule Deer	A	Uinta Ground Squirrel
*	Whitetail Deer	C	Red Squirrel
C	Moose	U	Northern Flying Squirrel
CY-RT	Pronghorn (Antelope)	C	Yellowbelly Marmot
CY-†T	Bison (Buffalo)	C	Pika
U	Bighorn Sheep	C	Northern Pocket Gopher
A	Coyote	A	Deer Mouse (White-footed Mouse)
*	Gray Wolf	U	Bushytail woodrat
R	Red Fox	C	Western Jumping Mouse
R	Bobcat	C	Richardson Vole
R	Lynx	C	Mountain Phenacomys
R	Mountain Lion (Cougar)	C	Boreal Redback Vole
U	Striped Skunk	A	Meadow Vole
C	Longtail Weasel	A	Mountain Vole
U	Shorttail Weasel (Ermine)	U	Longtail Vole
U	Mink	Rt	Sagebrush Vole
C	Marten	C	Masked Shrew
C	Badger	C	Vagrant Shrew
U	River Otter	U	Northern Water Shrew
*	Wolverine	Rt	Dwarf Shrew
U	Whitetail Jackrabbit	Ry	Dusky Shrew
C	Snowshoe Hare	C	Little Brown Myotis
Uy	Cottontail Rabbit	U	Long-eared Myotis
C	Porcupine	Ut	Long-legged Myotis
A	Beaver	Ry	Big Brown Bat
C	Muskrat	R	Silver-haired Bat
C	Least Chipmunk	RY-*T	Hoary Bat
		Ry	Western Big-eared Bat

(*Continued from page 145*)

shrew (commonly found in the subalpine and alpine areas), and the Northern water shrew (seldom found very far from the mossy banks of swift-flowing creeks in forest areas). The dwarf shrew, which weighs scarcely a tenth of an ounce, has been found in Grand Teton National Park, while the dusky shrew has been reported in Yellowstone.

THE BATS

Bats are the only mammals capable of true flight. The fore-limbs, modified as wings, consist of greatly elongated fingers that serve as a framework for a very thin membrane. The hind legs and the tail are also connected by a membrane. Until recently the navigating powers of bats were a mystery, as it is known that they can fly with ease in total darkness. Recent research has shown that while the bat is in flight it emits high-pitched sounds that bounce off surrounding objects. These echoes provide the bat with information regarding the location of objects with which it might collide and also probably the whereabouts of insects on which it feeds.

Seven species of bats and myotis have been recorded in the Teton-Yellowstone region. But, for the casual visitor, it is almost impossible to identify the different species.

BIRDS

A remark frequently heard from visitors in the Parks is that birds seem to be scarce in the Teton-Yellowstone region. That impression of scarcity is rather fallacious, though it does have some foundation. Most of the visitors come from sections of the country that are very much more settled. They are unused to bird-life conditions in places where wilderness surroundings so vastly predominate. In the settled parts of the country the birds have perforce grown accustomed to highways and to highway conditions of traffic; to cities and villages and everything that is associated

147

with proximity to civilization. In such parts of the country the bird life is more intimate, more familiar, so that the layman from a populous region acquires the impression that birds are inclined to be bold and confiding. The fact is, however, that birds are timid and retiring by nature; and that fact is well shown in such an area as Grand Teton and Yellowstone Parks where natural conditions prevail. If there are few birds seen on your motor tour of the Parks, as compared with the number which should be expected in an equally diversified ride in the country near a major city, it is largely because of the wilder places being available all about the Parks. In other words, the birds prefer wild conditions and in Teton-Yellowstone country such conditions are to be had in abundance. The birds do not have to dwell within the din and dust of traffic.

Another condition affects our bird life in a more fundamental way. The elevation of the Parks—approximately 5,000 to over 12,000 feet—does not favor maximum bird life, particularly as to the number of species. Lower altitudes, other conditions being equal, are richer in number of species. The bird life of Teton-Yellowstone region is, therefore, not remarkable for number of species or abundance of individuals in general. The most outstanding feature of its bird life, as a whole, is perhaps the fine representation it contains of species that are typical of the Rocky Mountain region.

For bird watching, as well as for spotting mammals, binoculars will be found useful. The Teton-Yellowstone region's bird population includes over two hundred species. The following list of birds of the Parks is based almost entirely on reported observations by members of the National Park Service and visiting ornithologists. The abundance of birds is indicated as common, occasional, or rare. Very rare or accidental species are marked by an asterisk. The times of abundance of the different bird species, of course, varies, and are indicated by seasons (Spring, Summer, Fall, Winter). The relative abundance symbols are general estimates listed merely to aid you in determining which species may be easily observed. The common species names used in this list are in accordance with Roger Tory Peterson's *Field Guide to Western Birds*. If you have any doubts or questions as to the possibility of a certain species of bird, discuss the matter with one of the Park Naturalists. Remember that the study of birds, as with all animals, calls for great patience, just a reasonable amount of caution, and, of course, common sense.

An eager beaver at work in the Grand Tetons.
Grand Teton Lodge Company Photo.

Trumpeter swans with four cygnets. One of the world's rarest birds, native only to North America. Adults weight 20-30 lbs., with a wingspread of over 7 feet. World's largest waterfowl. Have been known to live for over 30 years. Over half the U.S. population of species live in Grand Teton and Yellowstone.

Yellowstone National Park Photo.

CHECKLIST OF BIRDS FOUND IN GRAND TETON AND YELLOWSTONE NATIONAL PARKS

KEY:

Status	*Abundance*
S—March to May	C—common
S—June to August	O—occasional
F—September to November	R—rare
W—December to February	*—reported to be seen

Teton SSFW		Yellowstone SSFW
R R	Common loon	OOO
	Red throated loon	*
	Red necked grebe	*
*	Horned grebe	RR
R O	Eared grebe	CCC
R R	Western grebe	*
RRO	Pied-billed grebe	ROR
CRO	White pelican	CCO
R	Double-crested cormorant	R
CCCR	Great blue heron	CCCR
*	Common egret	*
*	Snowy egret	*
*	Black crowned heron	*
OO	American bittern	*
	Wood ibis	*
*	White-faced ibis	*
O OO	Whistling swan	C CC
CCCC	Trumpeter swan	CCCC
CCCC	Canada goose	CCCC
*	Snow goose	*
*	White-fronted goose	
COCR	Gadwall	CCCO
CCCC	Mallard	CCCC
COCO	Pintail	COCO
COCO	Green-wing teal	CCCO
ORR	Blue-wing teal	CCCO
RR	Cinnamon teal	RR
C CR	American widgeon	CRCO
R R	Shoveller	OOO
R R	Wood duck	R
O C	Redhead	O O
O OR	Ringneck	OOOR
R R	Canvasback	O O
	Greater scaup	CRCC
O O	Lesser scaup	C
O OO	Common goldeye	CRCC
CCCO	Barrow's goldeye	CCCC
O OO	Bufflehead	COCC
RRR	Harlequin duck	OOOR
	Whitewing scoter	*
	Common scoter	*
*	Ruddy duck	OR
RRRR	Hooded merganser	O
CCCC	Common merganser	CCCC
C C	Wilson's phalarope	COC
	Northern phalarope	R R
CCC	California gull	CCCR
RR	Ringbill gull	O
R	Franklin's gull	O
	Herring gull	*

Teton SSFW		Yellowstone SSFW
*	Bonaparte's Gull	*
*	Forster's tern	*
	Caspian tern	OOO
R R	Black tern	OR
	Common tern	*
OOO	Mourning dove	OOO
*	Yellow-billed cuckoo	
*	Black-billed cuckoo	*
OOOO	Screech owl	RRRR
CCCC	Great horned owl	OCOO
	Snowy owl	*
	Hawk owl	R
OOOO	Pygmy owl	RRRR
R	Burrowing owl	*
OOOO	Great gray owl	O O
RR	Longeared owl	RRRR
OOO	Shorteared owl	RORR
	Boreal owl	R
RRR	Saw-whet owl	OOO
RR	Poor-will	
CCC	Common nighthawk	O
RR	White throated swift	R
	Black swift	*
RR	Black-chinned Hummingbird	
OOO	Broad-tailed Hummingbird	R
OOO	Rufous Hummingbird	O
CCC	Calliope Humming-bird	O
OOOR	Belted kingfisher	OCOO
CCCR	Red-shafted flicker	CCCR
	Redheaded woodpecker	R
OOO	Lewis woodpecker	RR
CCC	Yellowbelly sapsucker	OO
OO	Williamson's sapsucker	CCC
CCCC	Hairy woodpecker	CCCO
CCCC	Downy woodpecker	CCCO
	Black-backed three-toed woodpecker	RRRR
RR	Northern three-toed woodpecker	OOOO
OOO	Eastern kingbird	OO
O	Western kingbird	R
	Cassin's kingbird	*
OO	Say's phoebe	O
CCC	Traill's flycatcher	O

Teton SSFW		Yellowstone SSFW
CCC	Hammond's flycatcher	O
OOO	Dusky flycatcher	OOO
	Western flycatcher	OOO
CC	Western Wood pee-wee	C
CC	Olivesided flycatcher	O
CCC	Yellow warbler	CCC
	Myrtle warbler	R
CCC	Audubon's warbler	CCC
RR	Townsend's warbler	O
R	Northern waterthrush	R
CCC	MacGillivray's warbler	O
CCC	Yellowthroat	O
*	Yellow-breasted chat	
OOO	Wilson's warbler	CCC
OOO	American redstart	
CCCC	English sparrow	OOOO
R R	Bobolink	O
CCC	Western meadowlark	CCCR
OOO	Yellow-headed blackbird	OO
CCC	Redwing blackbird	CCC
	Baltimore oriole	*
OOO	Bullock oriole	RR
CCC	Brewer's blackbird	CCCR
CCO	Brown-headed cowbird	OOOR
	Scarlet tanager	*
CC	Western tanager	CCC
CCO	Black-headed grosbeak	R
OO	Lazuli bunting	R
ORRO	Evening grosbeak	O
CCCO	Cassin's finch	CCC
OOOO	Pine grosbeak	OOOC
O OC	Gray-crowned rosy finch	O OC
COOC	Black rosy finch	O
	Turkey vulture	*
CCOO	Goshawk	O O
OOO	Sharp-skinned hawk	O O
OOO	Cooper's hawk	OOO
CCC	Redtail hawk	CCC
CCC	Swainson's hawk	CCC
CC	Roughlegged hawk	RRRO
RRR	Ferruginous hawk	R
OOOO	Golden eagle	CCCC
OOOO	Bald eagle	CCCC
CCCR	Marsh hawk	CCCR
CCCR	Osprey	CCC
OOO	Prairie falcon	R
*	Peregrine falcon	OO
*	Pigeon hawk	O
CCC	Sparrow hawk	CCC
OOOO	Blue grouse	CCCC
	Franklin's grouse	*
	Sharptail grouse	*
	White-tailed ptarmagin	RRRR
CCCC	Ruffed grouse	OOOO
CCCC	Sage grouse	RRRR
*	Hungarian partridge	*
*	Gray partridge	
OOO	Sandhill crane	CCC
*	Virginia rail	

Teton SSFW		Yellowstone SSFW
OOO	Sora	OO
CCC	American coot	CCC
CCC	Killdeer	CCC
RO	Mountain plover	*
	Black-belly plover	*
	Ruddy turnstone	R R
CCC	Wilson's snipe	OOO
OO	Longbill curlew	OO
CCC	Spotted sandpiper	CCC
CCC	Solitary sandpiper	C
OO	Willet	O
OO	Greater yellowlegs	OO
*	Lesser yellowlegs	O
*	Long-billed dowitcher	
	Pectoral sandpiper	R
	Baird's sandpiper	R
O	Least sandpiper	C
O	Western sandpiper	O
	Marbled godwit	RR
	Hudsonian godwit	R
	Sanderling	*
	Avocet	OOO
COOO	Horned lark	OCOO
CC	Violet-green swallow	CC
CC	Tree swallow	CC
CC	Bank swallow	CC
CC	Roughwing swallow	R
OOR	Barn swallow	OO
CC	Cliff swallow	CC
*	Purple martin	
CCCC	Gray jay	CCCC
CCCC	Steller's jay	CCCC
CCCC	Black-billed magpie	CCCC
CCCC	Raven	CCCC
R R	Western crow	RORO
R R	Pinon jay	*
CCCC	Clark's nutcracker	CCCC
CCCC	Black-capped chickadee	OCOO
CCCC	Mountain chickadee	CCCC
CCCC	White-breasted nuthatch	OOOO
OOOO	Red-breasted nuthatch	CCCC
	Pygmy nuthatch	*
CCCC	Water ouzel (dipper)	CCCC
CCOO	Brown creeper	OCOO
OOO	House wren	C
OO	Long-billed marsh wren	*
OO	Rock wren	OO
*	Mockingbird	*
*	Catbird	OO
OO	Sage thrasher	RR
CCC	Robin	CCCO
	Varied thrush	*
CC	Hermit thrush	CC
CC	Swainson's thrush	OO
	Veery	O
	Western bluebird	*
CCC	Mountain bluebird	CCC
CCCR	Townsend's solitaire	CCCO
OOO	Golden-crowned kinglet	R
OCO	Ruby-crowned kinglet	OCO
CCC	Water pipit	CCC
*	Sprague pipit	C C
	Bohemian waxwing	O C

(Continued)

Teton SSFW		Yellowstone SSFW	Teton SSFW		Yellowstone SSFW
OOO	Cedar waxwing	R	COC	Vesper sparrow	CCC
O CR	Northern shrike	C C		Sage sparrow	*
O O	Loggerhead shrike	R	R R	Slate-colored junco	
CCCR	Starling	OOOR	CCC	Oregon junco	CCCO
CCO	Warbling vireo	C	O O	Tree sparrow	OO
OOO	Orange-crowned warbler		CCC	Chipping sparrow	CCC
*	Nashville warbler	*	CCC	Brewer's sparrow	C
O O	Common redpoll	O		Harris' sparrow	*
COCO	Pine siskin	CCCO		Whitethroated sparrow	*
OOO	American goldfinch	OOO		Whitecrowned sparrow	CCC
OOO	Red crossbill	O O		Fox sparrow	R
	White crossbill	O	OOO	Lincoln's sparrow	OOO
CCC	Greentail towhee	OOO		Song sparrow	CCCO
*	Rufous-sided towhee	R	CCC	Lark sparrow	RR
RR	Lark bunting	O	OR	Snow bunting	O CC
COC	Savannah sparrow	CCC	O OO	Alaska longspur	O
	Grasshopper sparrow	R			

AMPHIBIANS AND REPTILES

Scarcely any reference need be made to the reptiles of the Parks because of the extreme paucity of their number. The Parks' long cold winters, high elevations, and short cool summers offer little encouragement to an animal that assumes the temperature of its environment. There are only five species of snakes reported in the Teton-Yellowstone region. Only one of these is poisonous and this, the prairie rattlesnake, occurs only in a couple of square miles in Yellowstone National Park, near the mouth of the Gardner River. They apparently do not exist in any area visited by tourists; thus you may enjoy whatever satisfaction there is in the fact that there are no poisonous reptiles in the Parks. In addition to snakes, there are a few lizards and toads, and an abundance of frogs. Here is a checklist of reptiles and amphibians of the Parks:

CHECKLIST OF REPTILES AND AMPHIBIANS FOUND IN GRAND TETON AND YELLOWSTONE NATIONAL PARKS

KEY: SEE page 146.

Abundance‡	Name	Abundance‡	Name
R	Rubber Boa	*	Short-horned Horned Toad
U	Western Garter Snake		
U	Common Garter Snake	C	Western Toad
Ry-*t	Bull Snake	A	Western Chorus Frog
Ry	Prairie Rattlesnake	C	Western Spotted Frog
Ry	Sagebrush Lizard	U	Leopard Frog
		C	Tiger Salamander

152

Chapter 8.

Fishing and Boating in the Parks

WATER sports of fishing and boating are popular with the visitors to Yellowstone and Grand Teton National Parks. In the case of fishing, for example, the National Park Service policy is to encourage the perpetuation of fish populations under natural conditions, while providing for recreational angling in unspoiled streams and lakes. That is, emphasis in the Parks is on affording you the thrill of real sport fishing in wild streams and lakes as a part of your total park experience, and not on providing large numbers of record-sized fish for the creel. But this does not mean that there are no line-snappers in the Parks' waters. There are plenty!

The waters of the Parks are really a fisherman's dream come true. Nearly all the streams and lakes contain one or more species of the following gamefish:

CUTTHROAT TROUT (*Salmo clarki lewisi*)

The cutthroat is the most widespread trout in the two Parks. Physically, this trout can be distinguished by a bright red or orange slash under his throat. Compared with other trout, his head is more pointed, his mouth somewhat larger in proportion. The black spots on the body are usually larger and less diffuse than on rainbow.

On rare occasions cutthroat, or native trout, weighing over 8 pounds have been caught in the Parks. The majority taken, however, weigh from about ½ pound to 4 pounds. Dry fly, wet fly, spinner, and bait are all used to catch them. Although a cutthroat is a splendid fighter, he seldom breaks water; he heads for the bottom when hooked and fights hardest when you bring him close, more dogged than brilliant in his tactics.

153

RAINBOW TROUT (*Salmo gairdneri irideus*)

Its name comes from the brilliant reddish "rainbow" streak found on its sides; but not all rainbows look alike. Some are nearly black and some are almost silver. They have black spots, too, but the spots are usually smaller than those on the cutthroat and their heads are spotted, too. Where rainbow and cutthroat inhabit the same waters they often interbreed to form a hybrid. The hybrid usually has most of the characteristics of rainbow, except that it frequently has the "cut throat" of the cutthroat trout.

For fly fishermen, the rainbow is the king of trout. They will often dash clear of the water to seize the fly and make repeated runs and leaps into the air after being hooked. They favor not only deep pools, but the long swift runs of a stream with moderate depth. When one is found working a riffle, there are probably others doing the same thing.

BROWN TROUT (*Salmo trutta fario*)

Often called the "Lock Leven," or the "German Brown" trout, this fish's general color has a more brownish or yellowish tinge than other trout of the Parks. Browns sometimes have a few spots on the upper edge of their tails, where other trout are spotted all over the tail. On brook trout the spots are rather faint. In lakes, browns may reach a weight of 20 pounds, but one pound is considered a good stream catch. They rise to a fly, but the larger ones are usually caught with bait or spinner near the bottom. When hooked it fights with anger but seldom with finesse.

BROOK TROUT (*Salevinus fontinalis*)

This trout is often considered one of the best tasting and beautiful fish that swims. Its back is dark olive to almost black. There are no spots on the back but there are wavy lines of lighter color that make it look vermiculated or marbled. The sides have red spots with blue borders, and the lower fins have a broad, white stripe along the entire forward edge. In the smaller streams of the Parks, the brook trout averages 8 to 10 inches, but in larger streams and in lakes, 12 to 15 inch specimens are fairly common.

The main characteristic of the "brookie" is viciousness. Not selective so much as it is greedy, so it is probably one of the easiest trout for the beginner to catch. While a fierce fighter, it does not break water. Preferring the calmer waters, usually the bigger the fish the deeper they will be.

GAMEFISH OF THE PARKS

Cutthroat Trout

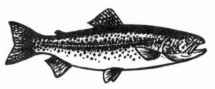

Rainbow Trout

Brook Trout

Lake Trout

Brown Trout

Grayling

Whitefish

LAKE TROUT (*Salvelinus namaycush*)

Here in the Parks, this species is known as the Mackinaw Trout. While its general color is lighter than the trout species previously mentioned, the Mackinaw may be greenish to grayish with many light spots on the sides. Some of the light spots on the back may be large and irregular, but they do not form vermiculations such as appear on the back of the brook trout. While the average lake trout is between 5 and 10 pounds, they often reach a weight of more than 30 pounds in Parks' waters, especially in Jackson Lake.

Mackinaw trout, as a rule, frequent deep, cold lakes. During the spring they may strike an artificial fly, but by far the greatest number are secured by deep trolling. Mackinaw may be caught through holes in the ice on Jackson Lake during the winter (see page 180).

GRAYLING (*Thymallus arcticus*)

This trout-shaped fish is best recognized by the large, sail-like back fin. Its general color is gray to silver with black spots, many of which are X-shaped. The eyes are large, but the mouth is small. Grayling are seldom found in Yellowstone waters larger than 15 inches long. They rise readily to an artificial fly, but are tricky to hook because of their small, tender mouth and their very agile movements.

MOUNTAIN WHITEFISH (*Coregonus williamsoni*)

The coloration of the mountain whitefish is quite ordinary, grayish blue above, silvery on the sides, a dull white below; no black spots. Average specimens taken in the Parks are about 12 inches long. Although they are basically bottom feeders, they break water to take surface insects and are occasionally hooked on a dry fly. Winter fishing for whitefish in Grand Teton National Park is becoming more popular each year (see page 180) and is a welcome diversion for the angler when he cannot enjoy his sport elsewhere.

There are other fish caught in the Parks in addition to the game species just described. These are the daces, sculpins, minnows, chubs, and suckers. They are all classed as non-game, or rough, fish and are seldom sought by the angler. There are no limits on the numbers of non-game fish that may be taken.

On facing page: *Fishermen coming to Grand Teton-Yellowstone area discover that fast-running streams and the crystal-clear glacial lakes are a haven for hard-fighting trout.*
Grand Teton Lodge Company Photo.

WHERE TO FISH

It is now generally recognized that Yellowstone and Grand Teton National Parks afford some of the finest trout fishing in the United States, if not the world. There are so many possibilities for every kind of fishing in these parks that the angler who wants to enjoy it to the fullest requires a variety of tackle. Of course, the visitor will normally seek the water best adapted to his favorite style of fishing, but he should be prepared to take advantage of the opportunities. Most successful methods, however, are fly, spinning, or trolling. As for the proper lures, bait, or flies, check with the park concessioners who operate the fishing tackle, boats and guide concessions.

YELLOWSTONE NATIONAL PARK

One of the most enjoyable aspects of Yellowstone Park waters is its variety—the angler can choose to fish anywhere from a tiny mountain pond to America's greatest fishing hole—the 139 square mile Yellowstone Lake. Or for stream fishing, he has a range from a calm meadow run, such as the Gibbon River, to a frothy backwater in the thundering Grand Canyon of the Yellowstone River. Actually Yellowstone's 440 miles of blue-ribbon trout streams and thousands of acres of blue alpine lakes offer some of the top fishing in North America.

Without question the easiest place in the Park to catch fish is at Yellowstone Lake, where even completely inexperienced fishermen can boat their limit of three trout, sometimes on the first three casts, or after a few minutes of trolling. (The latter is the most popular method of fishing on the Lake.) Aside from some nongame species, the only fish living in the Lake is cutthroat trout, and an average one measures about 13 to 16 inches.

By the way, boat rentals are available on the Lake at Fishing Bridge, Bridge Bay Marina, and West Thumb. Rowboats, outboards, and cabin cruisers afford the visitor a wide selection. Complete fishing tackle and bait can be rented or purchased at the boat docks. Also ask at these docks about guide service, which includes fishing boat, tackle, bait, and cleaning of fish.

From Yellowstone Lake the Park's mightiest river—the Yellowstone—begins its twisting race, through forest and canyon, to join the big Missouri, hundreds of miles distant to the north. The portion of the River in the Park annually yields thousands of cutthroats to fly and spin fishermen alike. Slough Creek, a tributary of the Yellowstone in the northeast corner of the Park, is another excellent cutthroat waterway. Of course, one of the most renowned

The boat marina at West Thumb of Yellowstone Lake.

World-famous fishing bridge at outlet of Yellowstone Lake.

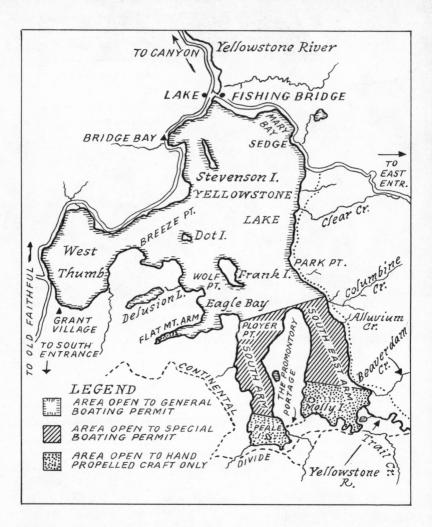

trout streams in the United States is the Madison River and it rises 14 miles west of Old Faithful Geyser in the Park. Along the Madison, the dry-fly fisherman has his heyday with browns and rainbows, which often reach record size.

One of the oddest trout streams in the world is the Firehole River, a tributary of the Madison. On either side of this river are boiling pools, geysers, and hot springs. Often the temperature of Firehole water rises above 80°, a temperature that is usually

---

On facing page: *Bridge Bay Marina. Launching ramp to left.*
Yellowstone Park Company Photo.

lethal to trout. However, possibly due to the high oxygen content of the water and the great amounts of food and vegetation, the fish can thrive next to hot steam vents that are submerged along the river's banks. Actually, for early summer fishing, the Firehole may be the best in the West. Most Western rivers are high and cold after the spring thaws. But the Firehole, warmed by geysers and hot springs, has fishing that is weeks ahead of the angling in other rivers. Hatches of insects come off early all along the upper Firehole. Even when the weather is unsettled and cold, the Firehole can provide unusual dry-fly fishing for browns and rainbow. Favorite flies in this area are the Muddler Minnow, Admos, Black Gnats, and Grizzly Wulff.

The Gibbon River, another Madison feeder stream, also offers excellent rainbow and brown fishing. Incidentally, roads parallel the Madison, Firehole, and Gibbon Rivers and the Yellowstone (above the Falls), making access a simple matter for motoring anglers. But, as previously mentioned, almost all the Park's streams and lakes provide topnotch fishing opportunities, and the following list shows the game fishes and the more important waters they inhabit:

Cutthroat Trout

Bechler River and
   Tributaries
Broad Creek
Cache Creek
Deep Creek
Gallatin River and
   Tributaries
Gardner River below
   the falls
Gibbon River
Hellroaring Creek

Lamar River
Lewis River
Middle Creek
Nez Percé Creek
Slough Creek
Snake River
Soda Butte Creek
Tower Creek
Yellowstone River
Beula Lake
Cascade Lake

Delusion Lake
Grebe Lake
Heart Lake
Lewis Lake
Mallard Lake
Riddle Lake
Shoshone Lake
Sportsman's Lake
Squaw Lake
Yellowstone Lake
   and Tributaries

Rainbow Trout

Firehole River
Gallatin River
Gardner River
Gibbon River
Hellroaring Creek
Iron Creek
Lamar River

Lewis River
Little Firehole
   River
Madison River
Middle Creek
Nez Percé Creek
Slough Creek

Soda Butte Creek
Tower Creek
Grebe Lake
Mammoth Beaver
   Dams
Sepulcher Lakes
Continued

On facing page: *Colter Bay Marina, Jackson Lake, Grand Teton.*
Union Pacific Railroad Photo.

Brown Trout

Firehole River
Gardner River below
   falls
Gibbon River

Iron Creek
Lewis River
Madison River
Nez Percé Creek

Sentinel Creek
Snake River
Lewis Lake
Shoshone Lake

Brook Trout

Blacktail Deer Creek
Gardner River above
   the falls
Gibbon River head-
   waters
Indian Creek

Obsidian Creek
Sentinel Creek
Solfatara Creek
Upper Firehole
   River

Upper Lava Creek
Grizzly Lake
Shoshone Lake and
   Tributaries

Lake (Mackinaw) Trout

Heart River
Snake River

Heart Lake
Lewis Lake

Shoshone Lake

Grayling

Gibbon River
Cascade Lake

Grebe Lake
Ice Lake

Wolf Lake

Mountain Whitefish

Hellroaring Creek
Gardner River

Lower Yellowstone
   River
Madison River

Slough Creek
Snake River

Several years ago officials at the Park introduced a new modification of the old sport—what they call "fishing for fun." Rules of the game are quite simple and include the following:

First, with a file or pliers, take the barb off your hook. You will lose plenty before you catch one, but that is the fun of it. When using barbed hooks, you usually land better than two of every three hooked.

Second, ethically you must release the first trout you net. There is the old superstition that releasing the first will much sweeten your luck.

Third, you keep any fish you hook hard. If he is hooked deep in the throat, through the gills or an eye, he is your fish.

Fourth, a fish fairly hooked and brought to the net must be released carefully. Using the barbless hook, this should be no problem.

Fifth, fish all day if you wish, but keep only a limit or the number you can actually use. It is better to return them for the next guy's fun. Who knows, you may be back again yourself.

GRAND TETON NATIONAL PARK

As in Yellowstone, there is a wide range of fishing opportunities. In Grand Teton National Park, an angler can try fly casting along a fast flowing mountain stream, trolling from a cabin cruiser, or drifting down the Snake River on a special six-man raft.

From May through June, the rivers and streams flow high and fast, filled with the melting waters of the winter snowpack. This is when Jackson, Jenny, and Leigh lakes are at their best, producing outstanding catches of Mackinaw and rainbow trout to the anglers who try their luck in the cool waters of the lakes. It is not uncommon for Mackinaw up to 30 pounds to be taken from the 400-foot depths of Jackson Lake. Deep water trolling is the common means of catching these lunker trout, and complete equipment including guide and boat may be rented at the Colter Bay Marina on the shore of Jackson Lake. Tackle may also be purchased or rented at the Marina, as well as at the Colter Bay Village Tackle Shop.

At Carmichael's Tackle Shop in Moose you can rent boats for deep water trolling on Lakes Taggart, Leigh, Jenny, and Lewis. Experienced guides at the shop will take you any place in Grand Teton National Park, or to their own favorite spots. Remember that every guide in the Park has gained firsthand knowledge of the means to successful fishing trips. Under Wyoming conservation law, which this Park follows, a guide must be a Wyoming resident for at least three years before qualifying for a guide license. The Park guides spend much time exploring the Jackson Hole country, discovering the most promising spots and most effective tackle—all to help visitors bring back limit catches on guided trips.

Bait and spin fishing is popular on the streams and rivers of Grand Teton throughout the summer and promises exciting fishing for rainbow, German Brown, and cutthroat trout. Fly fishing is ideal in the late summer and through September, since at this time of the year the fish group in deep holes and the water of the streams and rivers runs smooth and clear. The twisting Snake River provides some of the finest fly fishing anywhere in the Rocky Mountain area for scrappy cutthroat trout, and other areas such as the Buffalo River, Gros Ventre River, and Pacific Creek also provide excellent fishing. The favorite flies on these waters are the Mallard Spider, Mormon Girl, Buck Royal, and Blue Dun.

For an unusual fishing adventure, visitors try a challenging but safe 20-mile raft fishing trip down the Snake River, not to be confused with the famous Snake River float trip (see page 171). Carmichael's Tackle Shop offers this fishing trip daily, led by a guide. Large catches of cutthroat trout, the only trout native to Wyoming, are often taken. The Fish Hatchery near Jackson is open to the public and is of special interest to fishermen.

As mentioned before, almost all Park rivers, streams, and lakes provide excellent fishing opportunities, and here is a list of the game fish species available in the major waters:

Cutthroat Trout

Arizona Creek	Snake River	Jackson Lake
Berry Creek	Taggart Creek	Jenny Lake
Buffalo Fork River	Amphitheater Lake	Leigh Lake
Cascade Canyon Creek	Bearpaw Lake	Phelps Lake
Cottonwood Creek	Bradley Lake	Solitude Lake
Gros Ventre River	Emma Matilda	String Lake
Granite Canyon Creek	Lake	Surprise Lake
Lava Creek	Grizzly Bear Lake	Taggart Lake
Owl Creek	Holly Lake	Trapper Lake
Pacific Creek	Indian Lake	Two Ocean Lake
Phelps Lake Creek		

Rainbow Trout

Gros Ventre River	Jackson Lake	Leigh Lake
Snake River	Jenny Lake	

Brown Trout

Berry Creek	Snake River	Jackson Lake
Buffalo Fork River		

Brook Trout

Buffalo Fork River	Phelps Lake Creek	Jackson Lake
Cascade Canyon Creek	Snake River	Jenny Lake
Cottonwood Creek	Spread Creek	Leigh Lake
First Creek	Taggart Creek	Phelps Lake
Gros Ventre River	Bradley Lake	Taggart Lake
Pacific Creek		

Lake (Mackinaw) Trout

Snake River	Jenny Lake	Phelps Lake
Jackson Lake	Leigh Lake	

Mountain Whitefish

Buffalo Fork River	Phelps Lake Creek	Jenny Lake
Cottonwood Creek	Snake River	Leigh Lake
Gros Ventre River	Bradley Lake	Phelps Lake
Pacific Creek	Jackson Lake	Taggart Lake

166

FISHING REGULATIONS

The summary of the fishing regulations for the two parks below is furnished only for your guidance. Parkwide fishing regulations may be obtained at entrance stations or ranger stations, or from park rangers. They are changed from time to time; ignorance of them is not accepted as an excuse for violation. Fishing is permitted only with hook and line, with rod or line held in hand. Fishing from any bridge (except Fishing Bridge in Yellowstone) or boat dock is prohibited.

YELLOWSTONE NATIONAL PARK

No license is required to fish any of Yellowstone Park's waters. While some of the waters are closed to fishing—these are so designated by appropriate signs—remember that there are over 440 miles of streams that await the angler. The open season for fishing in the waters of the Park varies, but all close at sunset on October 31. Streams that open at sunrise on May 30 are: Yellowstone River and all tributaries below Upper Falls (Canyon), Firehole River and all tributaries below Old Faithful (fly fishing only), Gibbon River and all tributaries (fly fishing only below Gibbon Falls), Madison River and all tributaries (fly fishing only), Gardner River below water intake near Panther Creek, Lava Creek and the Lamar, Lewis, Snake, Gallatin Rivers and their tributaries. Slide, Lewis, Shoshone, Heart, Wolf, Riddle, and Grebe Lakes, plus the streams connecting Grebe and Wolf Lakes, open on this date also.

At sunrise, June 15, Yellowstone Lake (except the thermal area shoreline near West Thumb) and Squaw Lake (fly fishing only) will be open.

Open at sunrise, July 15, are all streams emptying into Yellowstone Lake, unless posted otherwise. Also open on this date is the Yellowstone River from its outlet at Yellowstone Lake to the Upper Falls, except from Alum Creek to Sulphur Cauldron which remains closed. This means fishing from famous Fishing Bridge is permitted from sunrise on July 15 to sunset on October 31. Fishing hours in the Park during the open season are: 4 a.m. to 9 p.m. from May 30 to August 31; 5 a.m. to 8 p.m. from September 1 to October 31. The use or possession of salmon, or any other fish eggs, minnows, or other bait fish—fresh or preserved—is prohibited. Digging of worms for bait is not permitted in the Park, but worms may be purchased at the boat docks on Yellowstone Lake.

Daily creel limits are as follows: Anglers on Yellowstone Lake and Yellowstone River (above Upper Falls) and its tributaries may keep a total of *three* fish. Anywhere else in the Park the maximum is *five* fish. Fish that are hooked and landed but are carefully handled and returned uninjured at once to the water are not to be considered in the catch or possession limit provided that at the time of catching and releasing, the angler has in possession no more than one fish less than the legal limit. He must cease fishing *immediately* upon filling his creel limit.

GRAND TETON NATIONAL PARK

A Wyoming State fishing license is required, and the general Wyoming fishing regulations apply within the Park, as well as certain special Park regulations. Fishing guides, boats, tackle and a State fishing license are available at the Park at Carmichael's Tackle Shop, Colter Bay Marina, Leek's Lodge, and Signal Mountain Lodge. Non-resident fishing licenses are $4.00 for a five-day permit and $12.00 for a season permit. (Children under 14 are not required to have a license but must be accompanied by an adult who has one.) The special Park regulations include the following:

Open Seasons (all dates inclusive):
> *Jenny* and *Leigh Lakes:* Open all year
> *Jackson Lake:* Open all year except October 1 through October 31
> *Snake River* and *all other Lakes:* April 1 through October 31
> *Other Streams:* June 1 through October 31
> *Snake River:* Whitefish only—open all year

Special Closures: The following waters are closed to fishing at all times:
> *Snake River:* From lower face of Jackson Lake Dam, 150 feet downstream.
> *Cottonwood Creek:* From Jenny Lake outlet to saddle horse concession bridge.
> *Swan Lake, Christian Ponds* and *Hedrick's Pond*

Creel Limits:
> *Jackson Lake:* 6 game fish, or 10 pounds and one fish (whichever is reached first) per day or in possession.
> *All Other Waters:* 12 game fish, or 10 pounds and one fish (whichever is reached first) per day or in possession. Whitefish limit to Snake River during open season is 25 per day with a possession limit of three days' catch.

The use or possession of fish eggs or fish for bait is prohibited in all Park waters, *except* that it is permissible to use and have in possession *dead* non-game fish for use as bait on or along the shores of Jackson Lake. Authorized bait dealers on Jackson Lake may hold, in containers removed from any fishing waters, live non-game bait fish taken from Jackson Lake, provided such fish are killed at time of sale.

BOATING IN THE PARKS

While most of the boats in use on Parks' water are used in conjunction with fishing, sceni-cruising and boat-camping have become very popular in recent years. Boats may be brought into the Parks or they may be rented at the various marinas on the major lakes. There are also several boating tours available.

YELLOWSTONE NATIONAL PARK

There are three lakes in Yellowstone on which boating is permitted: Yellowstone, Lewis, and Shoshone Lakes. But, Shoshone Lake, the Lewis River channel between Shoshone and Lewis Lakes, and portions of the three southern arms of Yellowstone Lake are open only to hand-propelled craft. A general permit is required for *all* boats operating upon the waters of the Park open to boating. A special permit is necessary for the zoned areas of South, Southwest, and Flat-Mountain Arms of Yellowstone Lake. These permits can be obtained free of charge at the following ranger stations: West Thumb, Lake, Bridge Bay, Fishing Bridge, South Entrance, and East Entrance.

Park regulations prohibit all privately owned boats more than 40 feet in length, sailboats, houseboats, and all water craft propelled by airplane-type propellers. (Also water skiing, boat racing, towing of aircraft, water pageants, and spectacular or unsafe types of recreational use are prohibited on all park waters.) Boats require a state or Coast Guard number, life jackets for all passengers, fire extinguisher, horn, bailing bucket, and the usual lights for night operation. Gasoline stoves cannot be used on board, and heads must have chlorinators or be sealed. Properly installed fuel tanks and backfire traps for inboards are other standard requirements. A complete boating regulation booklet may be obtained from any ranger station or the National Park Service, Yellowstone Park, Wyoming 83020. But, in general, these regulations parallel those of the Coast Guard or any state which complies with Federal Boating Act of 1958.

All boats 16 feet or less in length are prohibited a distance greater than one-quarter mile from the shore of any lake. This rule also applies to canoes, kayaks, and rafts, regardless of length. It is important to remember that a mountain lake like Yellowstone is subject to many moods, some of them bad. The pattern (subject to the usual vagaries of the weather) is for calm water from sundown to around 10:30 or so in the morning. Then a prevailing southwesterly comes up, blowing out of West Thumb and Flat Mountain Arm, to give the lake a steep short chop, uncomfortable for small craft. Although it usually takes twenty or thirty minutes for the water to get roiled, it can also snort up in short order. The water temperature averages around 41°, just nine above freezing. When a person is immersed in water below 68°, he loses heat faster than he manufactures it, and chilling sets in. Doctors estimate that the average person would be in serious trouble after an hour in these waters—hence the quarter-mile rule for small craft.

Although there are four launching ramps around Yellowstone Lake, the favorite of most boatmen is the new marina at Bridge Bay. This beautiful protected natural harbor has been dredged to 8 feet, equipped with floats, wide launching ramp, fuel dock, tackle shop, rest rooms, and ranger station. There is also a launching ramp at Lewis Lake. No charge is made for the use of any of the ramps.

Boat-camping and wilderness boating, as previously stated, have increased in recent years. There are over a half-dozen primitive marine campgrounds along the shores of both Yellowstone and Shoshone Lakes. (These campgrounds are accessible only by trail or by boat.) When you get your boat and fire permits, the ranger will gladly show you their locations.

While visiting wilderness areas of the Upper Yellowstone Lake is most interesting, possibly the ideal trip for the average canoeist (a canoe is the best boat for wilderness country) is the 7-mile voyage from Lewis Lake to Shoshone Lake. The approach is from the road at Lewis Lake, thence 3 miles west along the lake shore and 4 miles north up the Lewis Lake channel to Shoshone proper. Although the last three-quarters of a mile is a portage or hand-line tow over the rugged stream bed to Shoshone outlet, paddling up Lewis River to this point is a most enjoyable experience. It takes the average person about three or four hours to reach Shoshone Lake by canoe, depending on experience, load, weather, and the season of the year. Four days allotted to a trip around the lake is plenty of time to get a good idea of its wilderness values. In this amount of time you can visit the geyser basin at the extreme southwest end of the lake, a highlight of any trip. Even if your time is limited, twelve hours will give you a solid sample of Shoshone, and the gay ride down Lewis River rapids, fast but not hazardous as rapids go, is a thrilling climax in a pleasant day.

Boats may be rented at any of three boat rental docks on the Yellowstone Lake for those who wish to cruise along on its cobalt-blue waters. Or you may take the 40-passenger excursion boat that leaves Bridge Bay Marina on a regular schedule for a sceni-cruise of the Lake. The special twilight cruise of this vessel is especially interesting since you can usually see elk and moose browsing along the pine-clad coves of the lake.

GRAND TETON NATIONAL PARK

Motorboats may be operated by visitors only on Jackson, Jenny, and Phelps Lakes. (Phelps Lake may be reached only by trail, and motors over 7½ horsepower cannot be used on Jenny Lake.) Hand-propelled craft may be used on Jackson, Jenny, Phelps, Taggart, Bradley, Bearpaw, Leigh, String, Emma Matilda, and Two Ocean Lakes, and on the Snake River. All other lakes, streams, and ponds in the Park are closed to boating. Marinas at Jackson Lake offer a wide variety of boating services and facilities—including mooring and docking—and are located at Colter Bay, Signal Mountain Lodge, and Leek's Lodge. Boats may be launched at these locations, also there is a ramp at Jenny Lake. Boats may be rented at the Colter Bay Marina.

Grand Teton National Park boat permits, which are free, are required for all waterborne craft used in the Park. Regulations concerning permits, boat numbering, equipment, rules of the road, prohibited operations, and accident reporting requirements are available at all ranger stations, or from the National Park Service, Moose, Wyoming 83012. Like Yellowstone, these regulations follow the Federal Boating Act regulations. Private boats larger than 40 feet are prohibited in the Park, but sailboats may be used on Jackson Lake. Water skiing is also permitted on this lake.

One of the most exciting, yet safe, boating experiences in the Grand Tetons is the famous Snake River Float Trip. This voyage begins with a short bus ride from Jackson Lake Lodge, to a departure area on the banks of the smooth-flowing Snake River where passengers are seated in large rubber floats, each holding eighteen persons. After pushing off from shore, *expert* boatmen work large wooden sweeps or paddles that are attached to the front and rear of the floats and guide the floats down the river, taking their travelers through many miles of primitive landscape that is completely untouched by the technology of man. Once in the main current of the river and around the first bend of the Snake, passengers feel as if they are entering into another world, and the

171

mechanical sounds of everyday life are replaced with the gurgle of water and an occasional splash of a trout breaking the surface of the river. There will be some swift water as you cruise among the sandbars, and, by the time you stop for lunch at Deadman's Bar, the bluffs along the river will have become higher and your raft will have increased its speed considerably.

After lunch the floats again move out into the current of the river and enter the Snake River Canyon for the final leg of the journey. The last half of the trip is more brisk than the morning, and the floats pass quickly by huge granite boulders and thickly forested river banks. Towards the end of the day, as the shadows begin to lengthen over the river, the trip ends at Menor's Ferry. Here the floats are beached on the gravel bottom of the river and buses are waiting for the return to Jackson Lake Lodge. Reservations for this float trip can be made at the Transportation Desk of Jackson Lake Lodge or at Colter Bay Village. Other float trips on the Snake River can be arranged at Carmichael's Tackle Shop, or through the Jackson Hole Chamber of Commerce in Jackson.

Floating the Snake in privately owned craft can also be accomplished provided the proper precautions are taken in advance, safe equipment is used, and you are *fully* aware of the hazards that exist and may be encountered by *inexperienced* boatmen. You are urged to obtain the latest information regarding river conditions from the Chief Ranger's Office at the time you obtain a boat permit or prior to each float trip. Boat permits are required for all floating objects used to float the Snake River. Camping and picnicking ashore, when traveling by boat, are restricted to designated sites. A campfire permit must be obtained if a fire is planned.

Another enjoyable boat trip—either aboard your own boat, a rented one, or as a passenger aboard a sceni-cruiser—is the cruise around Jackson Lake. This takes you to the far shore, where you look deep into the wilderness country of canyons yet unmarked by trails, of mountains without names. On moonlit nights, there are picnic cruises, with campfire suppers on one of the islands. The moon behind these jagged peaks outlines each one in dramatic silhouette. Reservations for the various Jackson Lake cruises can be made at Colter Bay Marina or the Jackson Lake Lodge.

Boat trips are available at Jenny Lake, or you may rent a boat there. Such arrangements can be made at the Jenny Lake Lodge.

On facing page: *The float trip on Snake River, Grand Teton.*
Union Pacific Railroad Photo.

Yellowstone National Park Photo.

Winter snows are deep in Yellowstone as seen by the amount on campers' cabins at Old Faithful.

Chapter 9.

Winter Comes to the Parks

THE peak of the tourist season at the two parks is the six-week period of July 4 to August 15—but it remains busy and rather crowded to about August 25. Accommodations within the Parks begin opening up in May, and close down gradually as traffic dies out between Labor Day and early October. Actually, the Parks are often at their best in "off-seasons" of May-June and September-October.

In May and June, snow still graces most of the mountain peaks quite thickly, contrasting them sharply against the deep blue of early-summer skies. In September and early October, the aspen trees and other plant-life turn beautiful colors. The cooler atmosphere of the early and late season condenses a great deal of vapor over and around Yellowstone's geysers, hot springs and fumaroles, thus making them usually more highly photogenic. Also in spring and fall, wildlife becomes more in evidence. Deer, elk, moose, bison, and a myriad of smaller animals seem oblivious to man as they graze among the forest glades. Many fishermen find September the best month for fishing in Yellowstone and Teton country. Then the water has lowered and the fish begin to group in the deep holes. Of course, one of the major advantages of "off-season" travel in the Parks is that there are no time-wasting waits in traffic or in dining rooms, and it is no problem to get accommodations you wish. But once snow starts to fall, the Parks change. Let us see what they are like during the winter.

YELLOWSTONE'S WINTER WONDERS

There are two faces to Yellowstone National Park. We all know the warm-weather face of the Park. The second is little known and is seen by only an infinitesimal fraction of the total number of park visitors. In winter, of course, heavy snows sweep

175

across the Continental Divide and most park entrances are closed.

From Gardiner to Mammoth Hot Springs, and from Mammoth across the northern part of the Park to Northeast Entrance and Cooke City, Montana, the road is open all winter. Beyond Cooke City, however, the road is closed from approximately October 15 to June 1, so the Northeast Entrance is, in effect, closed during this period. West, East and South Entrances are closed from approximately November 1 to May 1. Obviously, it would be economically impractical to clear the 30-foot-high snowbanks from such places as Dunraven Pass to accommodate a few tourists even if the plows could buck Yellowstone's windswept drifts. However, development of tractor-tread snowmobiles in the past dozen years, along with smaller, faster snowplanes, has opened some of this wonderland to winter visitors.

The Mammoth Motor Inn is open throughout the entire year and snowmobiles take visitors to various points of interest. Park Headquarters at Mammoth Hot Springs also remain open. A few rangers are sprinkled about other sectors of the Park and are linked by two-way radio and telephone with Park Headquarters.

The second entry point for trips into Yellowstone during snow season is West Yellowstone, Montana, traditionally one of the most frigid spots in the nation. Temperatures drop to the below-zero mark most nights, and during a cold spell, readings of minus 30° are commonplace. Old-timers recall that a record low of 69° below zero was registered on the town's uncracked thermometers back in February, 1933, and even prideful natives admit that that was a fairly chilly occasion. However, high-altitude sun will warm winter visitors, and snow-touring equipment now in use is surprisingly comfortable. Nevertheless, it is obviously logical to pack plenty of warm clothing, including long underwear of the type favored by skiers and ranchers, before venturing on a snow-season junket into Yellowstone.

The approved Park Service-licensed method of witnessing winter in Yellowstone is by means of snowmobiles operated from West Yellowstone and Mammoth. The rates are reasonable for these junkets, and children under 12 travel for half fare. Perhaps more important in this country, the vehicles carry an emergency food supply and have two-way radio communication with their home bases of operation. A country in which nights are always frigid, and in which storms can drop a foot of wind-driven snow in a few hours, is not country for poorly equipped vehicles or amateur drivers.

A typical trip aboard one of these snowmobiles takes winter visitors from West Yellowstone to Madison Junction across a

176

portion of the Madison Plateau country that was fractured several years ago by an earthquake. Then the vehicles clatter on south past Fountain Paint Pot and Lower Geyser Basin to Old Faithful, a distance of approximately 30 miles. Operating strictly by Park Service and Interstate Commerce Commission rules, the 10-passenger vehicles stick to the snow-covered highway as much as possible even though the pavement, posts, and signs are rarely visible. While the interior of the snowmobiles is heated and reasonably comfortable, travelers should wear ski pants, parkas, and hiking boots, since deep snow will be encountered at stopovers, except in the naturally heated lea of some geysers and "hot spots."

Basically, winter vacationists taking the snow trips will find two major attractions—plentiful wildlife and plentiful scenery. Obviously, not one of the snowmobile drivers can guarantee the presence of big game on every trip, but it is a really rare day when visitors fail to spot buffalo, elk, and wildfowl. Several hundred elk and buffalo herd up in the countryside passed by the snowmobiles, and drivers will readily halt at the request of amateur naturalists and photographers. Usually, a few Canada geese and even a trumpeter swan or two will choose to winter along nearby streams, apparently seeking out the warm pools. Ducks are plentiful, deer turn up toward sundown, and coyotes, rabbits, and such furbearers as mink, marten, and otter often can be spotted. Yellowstone bears are in their winter sleep, of course, although rangers sometimes report a wintertime stroller or two.

The major attraction of a Yellowstone snow-season trip, aside from the strikingly beautiful, untracked, empty character of high-altitude, forested countryside, is the strange, eerie quality of the most familiar thermal features of the park when viewed in a deep-snow, low-temperature setting. Old Faithful's plume of water and steam, and the spray from other erupting geysers in the nearby basins, all seem far more intense against winter skies, and there is an odd quality to heavy clouds rising over the pools and above the Firehole River that is difficult to describe. Actually, the snowmobile trips are adventures into an oddly unreal world. Snow and ice creep close to steam pots and geysers. The steamy hot water showering down from erupting geysers builds windrows, ledges, and a multitude of other ice formations downwind from the high-temperature areas. Snow builds up upon the ice, spray falls upon trees, fostering still other odd formations. Meantime, deep snow mantles spruce and pine forests until boughs creak under its weight. Aside from the sound of snowmobile engines and tractor-like treads, there is a hushed quality in wintertime Yellowstone. When drivers shut off engines, the silence is broken only by the occasional cry of a bird or coyote, the sifting of snow from a bough or the gurgling of the water in an unfrozen stream or steaming paint-pot.

Old Faithful Motor Lodge, like Mammoth Motor Inn, is operated the year 'round. This makes it possible for visitors either to stay overnight in the Park or return the same day to West Yellowstone. Overnight accommodations can be had at the motels and lodges which remain open in town during the winter. In summertime, when the community swarms with visitors, motels and lodges are usually overcrowded, but during the cold weather visitors can find good accommodations with no difficulty. An increasing number of skiers from the Butte and Helena areas, and from southern Idaho and Utah cities, have been coming to the West Yellowstone country for such change-of-pace winter sport, and are combining skiing with snowmobile junkets.

Roads into West Yellowstone are kept open by state highway crews, although blizzards occasionally cut off the country for a day or so. A daily bus service from Ashton, Idaho, and another bus route from Bozeman, Montana, are the only means of entry for visitors lacking automobile transportation. However, some eager winter scenery-seekers have lately been flying to Idaho Falls, and renting cars there for the West Yellowstone journey. The road into Gardiner from the north is kept open throughout the year.

WINTER GRANDEUR IN THE GRAND TETONS

Grand Teton National Park, unlike Yellowstone, is *officially* open during the snow season. Actually, the National Park Service encourages winter-use programs such as informal skiing, snowshoeing, skating, and tobogganing. At the present time the most active winter use of the Park is on Jackson Lake where snowplaning and fishing through the ice are popular throughout the winter months or as long as the ice is safe, usually until about April 1. Winter mountaineering and ski touring are increasing in popularity within the Park, but require official ranger permission the same as for summer mountaineering (see page 115).

Just outside the Park, 7 miles from Moose on the Moose-Wilson road, the winter visitor can find one of the United States' largest ski developments. This area now features a 2,000-foot double chairlift and 2½-mile, 63-passenger, jig-back aerial tram with a vertical rise of 4,135 feet, the largest ski area tramway on the continent. (The tram is operated in the summer, too.) Eventually, this ski complex will feature five double chairlifts, three four-passenger gondolas, and a complete alpine village with guest chalets, restaurants, ski shops, and homesites.

Another popular area is Snow King Mountain, just south of Jackson, and it features a 1,571-foot vertical drop, excellent trails

178

Yellowstone National Park Photo.

The Grand Canyon of the Yellowstone and
Lower Falls from Artist Point in the winter.

for the advanced beginner, intermediate, and expert skier, and a 40-meter jump. Serviced by a 4,000-foot double chairlift and three rope tows, it has an excellent certified ski school. (The chairlift is also operated in summer for those who want a spectacular view of the surrounding countryside.) A public lodge, eating facilities, and skating rink are located at the base of the mountain. Another spot a few miles west of Jackson, Teton Pass, is a favorite area for the powder enthusiasts, who can often enjoy excellent snow conditions from November on.

The Rocky Mountain whitefish is the species sought after during the winters in the Snake River while Mackinaw Trout keep anglers happy on Jackson Lake. Types of tackle and bait will vary, so it is best to follow the advice given by the sporting goods stores in Jackson. The whitefish season is open year around with a twenty-five-fish limit and seventy-five fish in possession. Mackinaw limits are the same as in the summer months (page 168). A Wyoming fishing license is required, and while you are purchasing the license, check the fishing regulations for closed waters.

While wildlife abounds in the Park for visitors to view during the winter months, one of the two largest native elk herds in the United States has its winter range on the National Elk Refuge, a 25,000-acre plot which forms the southeastern boundary of Grand Teton National Park. Thousands of elk can be seen from the highway on the western edge of the Refuge. One of the most interesting highlights of a winter trip to the Tetons is being able to drive out among the herd of some seven thousand to nine thousand elk on the horse-drawn feed sleds to take pictures and observe the animals close-up. The public is invited to ride the sleds, which leave from the first group of buildings and hay sheds seen just after entering the Refuge.

As the winter months approach, the Yellowstone Park Road is the first to close. Usually by October 15 or shortly afterwards "road closed" signs are placed at the junction near Buffalo Junction and at Jackson Lake Lodge. As the snow moves down into the valley, all roads in the Park except the few that are kept open all winter, close to travel so that by early December travel anywhere, except on plowed roads must be by snowplane, skis, or snowshoes. The main highway from the south boundary of the Park to the northeast boundary and which continues over Togwotee Pass, and northwest as far as Jackson Lake Ranger Station and Jackson Lake Dam is kept open all winter, as are roads in and around Park Headquarters, the Wilson Road to the JY Ranch, the road to Kelly and north to Antelope Flats and back to Jackson Hole Highway. A few other short roads into occupied ranches are kept open; otherwise, over-snow equipment is required for travel.

The snowplane is becoming ever more popular as a means of seeing and enjoying the Park in winter. As a result, a permit system has been initiated whereby snowplane operators are required to register their planes at Park Headquarters or Jackson Lake Ranger Station before venturing into the Park.

While snowmobiles similar to those used in Yellowstone make daily trips to Teton Park from Jackson and travel at a respectable gait of 30 miles per hour or thereabouts, they should not be confused with snowplanes. The latter are, in effect, sleds powered by airplane-type propellers. Some snowplanes, as previously stated, are available on an individual charter basis for runs into portions of Grand Teton National Park and the southern reaches of Yellowstone. While faster, they are not so comfortable as the tracked vehicles.

During the winter months the only way of reaching the Park other than by automobile is to come in by plane. Bus lines, at the present time, do not operate, and there is no train service. A commercial line, Frontier Airlines, private planes, and charter flights operate in and out of Jackson airport daily, weather permitting. When driving an automobile, remember that anyone using mountain roads in the winter should always be prepared for the worst. Being prepared means good reinforced chains, tires with good tread, a snow shovel, heater and defroster in good condition, windshield wipers that sweep clean, a well-charged battery that will start the vehicle in coldest weather, and the motor in good condition. A word of caution about chains: chains do often give the additional traction needed on icy or snow-packed roads, but remember that even with the best reinforced chains it requires three times more distance to stop than on dry pavement. Also, when you feel chains are needed it is best to put them on before you find yourself possibly stuck in a hazardous spot. And you will find it much easier to put them on before rather than after you get stuck.

Approximately 250 inches of snow is received during a year; snow depth in the Moose, Jenny Lake, and Jackson Lake areas averages 5 to 6 feet.

Concession facilities within the Park are closed usually around October 1 and do not open until late May to mid-June. Accommodations are available the year around in nearby Jackson. Several private operations in and near the Park provide accommodations slightly earlier and later than the concessioners. During the winter the ranger force is stationed at Park Headquarters in Moose and at the Jackson Lake Ranger Station.

Chapter 10.

Accommodations and Services in the Parks

A CCOMMODATIONS in both Yellowstone and Grand Teton National Parks are as varied as the scenery. You can find an old-fashioned charm at historic Old Faithful Inn, or a rich striking feeling of modern beauty at Jackson Lake Lodge. For those who really want to "rough-it" there are campers' cabins and tent villages. Between these extremes the range of lodging is wide, at prices that seem reasonable, all things considered. Speaking of rates, they have been omitted in this chapter, since they may change during the operating season. But, remember the rates of park concessioners are subject to National Park Service approval.

YELLOWSTONE NATIONAL PARK

The Yellowstone Park Company, long associated with the history and growth of the Park, operates hotels and lodges, cottages and cabins, dining rooms and cafeterias, boats, horseback trips, and buses. Credit cards of the American Express Company are honored at all their hotels, lodges, and cabin offices.

Although there are over nine thousand varied accommodations in Yellowstone (this does not include campsites), it is advisable to request reservations in advance through a travel agent or write directly to the Yellowstone Park Company, Reservations Department, Yellowstone National Park, Wyoming 83020. (Deposits—usually one day's rent—are ordinarily required.) A complete schedule of rates for the following classifications of accom-

On facing page: *Old Faithful Geyser and Inn, from Observation Point.*
Union Pacific Railroad Photo.

modations will be sent on request by Yellowstone Reservations Department:

Hotel or *Inn Room*. Steam heated, with or without private bath.

Hotel Cottages. Heated by gas or by wood-burning stoves, hot and cold running water, with or without private bath.

Lodge Cabins. Heated by gas or by wood-burning stoves, hot and cold running water, with or without private bath; grouped near central building housing registration office, restaurant, and allied service. No cooking permitted in lodge cabins.

Campers' Cabins. Heated by individual wood-burning stoves; may be rented with or without bedding or fuel. Cooking permitted; guests should bring own utensils or purchase locally.

Unless you are thoroughly familiar with the several major areas of the Park, you will not know in advance how to divide your time, so firm reservation at one location for entire stay is not always the best idea. It is usually better to make reservations at one spot for the first couple of days and then decide, soon after you arrive, where you wish to visit next, and ask your desk clerk to get you space there. If you have no advance reservations at all, you can stop at the Yellowstone reservation booths in Billings and West Yellowstone (Montana), and Cody, Jackson Lake Lodge and Mammoth Motor Inn (Wyoming) for assistance. Accommodations are available at the following major locations in the Park:

Mammoth Area

Mammoth Motor Inn. Hotel rooms and cottages; dining room, coffee shop, snack bar and cocktail lounge. Season: Hotel rooms are available the year 'round; cottages from June 10 to Sept. 1.

Canyon Area

Canyon Village Motor Lodge. Modern motel-type units; dining room, coffee shop, cafeteria, and cocktail lounge. Season: Approximately May 27 to September 6.

Old Faithful Area

Old Faithful Inn. Hotel rooms; dining room, coffee shop and cocktail lounge. Season: From approximately May 15-Oct. 10.

Old Faithful Motor Lodge. Dormitory-type rooms; campers' cafe, and tap room. The Motor Lodge facilities are available the year 'round.

Old Faithful Lodge. Cabins; dining room. Season: From about June 10-Sept. 10. *Campers' cabins* open from about May 15-Oct. 15.

On facing page: *Aerial view of Lake Hotel, Yellowstone Park.*
Yellowstone Park Company Photo.

184

Lake Area

Lake Hotel. Hotel rooms and cottages; dining room and cocktail lounge. Season: Hotel rooms from about June 5 to September 10; cottages from approximately June 1 to September 10. *Lake Lodge.* Cabins; cafeteria. Season: From about May 15 to October 1.

Roosevelt Lodge Area

Roosevelt Lodge. Cabins; dining room. Season: Approximately June 15 to September 1.

West Thumb Area

West Thumb Campers' Cabins. Campers' cabins; cafeteria. Season: About June 10 to September 10.

Fishing Bridge Area

Fishing Bridge Campers' Cabins. Campers' cabins; cafeteria. Season: About May 28 to September 10.

Outside the Park's boundaries, accommodations are available in West Yellowstone, Gardiner, Silver Gate, Cooke City(Mont.), and Cody (Wyo.).

GRAND TETON NATIONAL PARK

Major facilities in the Park are operated by the Grand Teton Lodge Company, owned by Jackson Hole Preserve, Inc., a non-profit educational and conservation organization. It operates:

Jackson Lake Lodge. Hotel rooms with private bath and modern motel-type cottages; dining room, fountain room, and cocktail lounge. Season: The first week in June to the third week in September.

Jenny Lake Lodge. One- and two-room rustic cottages with all modern comforts; dining room (modified American plan—breakfast and dinner). Season: Approximately June 15 to September 10.

Colter Bay Cabins. One- and two-room cabins with private baths; tap room, cafeteria and grill. Season: About May 28 to October 1.

Colter Bay Tent Village. Tent shelters equipped with outdoor grill, wood-burning stove, table and benches, and two double-

On facing page: *Grand Teton Lodge, with mountain range visible in background.*

Grand Teton Lodge Company Photo.

decker bunks without bedding. Other housekeeping furnishings are available for rental. Season: From approximately June 15 to September 15.

Write to the Grand Teton Lodge Company for reservations and rates: summer address, Jackson, Wyoming 83001; Winter address, 209 Post Street, San Francisco, California 94108.

The following are other concessioners within the Park that have accommodations available:

Elbo Ranch, Kelly, Wyoming (3.7 miles north of Moose Junction). Cabins with meals; saddle horses for ranch guests.
Leek's Lodge, Moran, Wyoming (on Jackson Lake 5.7 miles north of Jackson Lake Junction). Cabins, dining room, boats, fishing tackle, and gasoline.
Signal Mountain Lodge, Moran, Wyoming (on Jackson Lake 2.9 miles south of Jackson Lake Junction). Cabins, dining room, store, soda fountain, boats, gasoline.
Triangle X Ranch, Moose, Wyoming (East side of Snake River, 9 miles north of Moose). Cabins, dining room, and lounge in main ranch house. An operating cattle ranch.

There are also accommodations within the boundaries of the Park which are on privately owned property. The policies and practices of private operators are *not* subject to the rules and regulations of the National Park Service. In addition, there are all types of accommodations in and near the town of Jackson. Write to the Jackson Hole Chamber of Commerce, Jackson, Wyoming 83001, for their directory of motels, hotels, dude ranches, and other resorts in the area including the private operators within the Park. The Chamber (one block north of Jackson Square) remains open until late evening to assist visitors in finding accommodations.

CAMPGROUNDS

In both Parks, campground is an area with an organized layout having well-defined roads, parking spaces, and campsites. Drinking water and sanitary facilities, including toilets and refuse cans, are furnished on a community basis. Each campground has a designed capacity based on the number of campsites therein. (The exception to this is an overflow area which will crowd in as many campers as possible for an overnight stay.) A campground site, or campsite, is a clearly marked plot or location within a campground which provides accommodations for camping by an individual, family, or party. A typical campsite in a campground generally includes a parking space, fireplace, table and bench combination, and a tent space; however, in a walk-in campground or walk-in section of a campground, the parking space is provided but not as an integral part of each campsite.

In each park arrangements can be made for organized group camping such as Boy Scouts, school group, or other large parties. Since these arrangements require advanced planning, reservations are mandatory. Request should be sent as much in advance of the trip as possible. Write to the Superintendent, Yellowstone Park, Wyoming 83020; or Superintendent, Grand Teton National Park, Moose, Wyoming 83012.

The use of all *public* campgrounds in the Parks is on a "first come—first served" basis, with the exception of organized group camping. In most cases, campers should arrive early in the day, preferably *before* noon. No fee is charged for use of campgrounds; reservations are not made.

YELLOWSTONE NATIONAL PARK

There are eighteen improved camp and trailer grounds inside the Park. Trailers are permitted in all of the campgrounds listed below. However, there are no electrical or plumbing hook-ups, nor are shower facilities available. In addition to those listed, there are other designated sites scattered through the Park for hikers, horseback parties, or people using boats (see Chapter 5). For these remember that a campfire permit is required. Otter Creek and Indian Pond are the two group camping areas in the Park while Whiskey Springs is the overflow campground.

Name and Location	No. Camp Sites	Season	Piped Water	Toilet
Bridge Bay 3.8 mi. S. W. of Lake Junction	230	6/1-10/15	Yes	Flush
Canyon Canyon Village	340	6/1-9/15	Yes	Flush
Fishing Bridge 0.8 mi. E. of Lake Junction	317	6/1-9/15	Yes	Flush
Grant Village 1.6 mi. S. of West Thumb	399	6/1-9/30	Yes	Flush

(*Continued*)

Name and Location	No. Camp Sites	Season	Piped Water	Toilet
Indian Creek 8.1 mi. S. Mammoth Hot Springs	78	6/1-9/1	Yes	Pit
Lava Creek 4.3 mi. E. Mammoth Hot Springs	10	5/15-9/15	No	Pit
Lewis Lake 8.3 mi. S. West Thumb	100	6/1-10/31	Yes	Pit
Madison Junction 13.9 mi E. North Entrance	300	6/1-9/15	Yes	Flush
Mammoth 4.4 mi. S. of North Entrance	91	4/15-10/31	Yes	Flush
Norris 20.4 mi. S. Mammoth	116	6/15-9/10	Yes	Flush
Old Faithful 16.2 mi. S. Madison Junction	323	5/1-10/15	Yes	Flush
Pebble Creek 9.9 mi. S.E. Northeast Entrance	36	6/1-9/15	Yes	Pit
Pelican Creek 1.7 mi. E. of Lake Junction	111	7/1-8/15	Yes	Pit
Slough Creek 6.4 mi. E. of Tower Junction	26	6/1-9/1	No	Pit
Snake River South Entrance	20	6/10-9/1	Yes	Pit
Specimen Creek 26 mi. N. of West Entrance	19	6/1-9/1	No	Pit
Tower Fall 2.6 mi. S. of Tower Junction	53	6/1-9/15	Yes	Pit

NOTE: During the period from June 30 through Labor Day camping in the Park is limited to a total of 14 days; otherwise 30-day limit.

In addition, the concessioner-operated Fishing Bridge Trailer Park has 358 house-trailer sites with water, sewer, and power hook-ups. A charge is made per day. Laundromat facilities, showers, and hair dryers are available at nominal rates. June 15-September 15. Length of stay limited to fourteen days. Reservations of trailer sites advisable. Write to Hamilton Stores, Inc., West Yellowstone, Montana 59758.

GRAND TETON NATIONAL PARK

Main campgrounds are noted below. Trailers permitted in all campgrounds except Jenny Lake; no utilities or services available. Out-camping is permitted in certain back-country locations (see page 111).

Name and Location	No. Camp Sites	Camping Limit	Piped Water	Toilet
Colter Bay E. shore of Jackson Lake, Colter Bay	365	14-Day	Yes	Flush
Jackson Lake 3.1 mi. S. of Jackson Lake Junction	100	14-Day	Yes	Pit
Jenny Lake 7.3 mi. N. of Park Headquarters	85	10-Day*	Yes	Pit
Gros Ventre Area 4 mi. E. on Gros Ventre-Kelly Road	214	14-Day	Yes	Flush
Lizard Point 13 mi. N. of Jackson Lake Junction	60	14-Day	Yes	Flush

* A special Climber's Campground, with 14-day limit between June 20 and August 31, is located on the south shore of Jenny Lake and has been set aside *solely* for mountain climbers' use. It is the duty of registration rangers (see page 115) to supervise this camping area and enforce all regulations concerning it.

In addition, the concessioner-operated Colter Bay Trailer Village has 112 house trailer sites with power, water, and sewer connections. The charge is made per day. Advance reservations of sites is advisable. Contact the Grand Teton Lodge Company. See page 188 for address.

GENERAL RULES FOR CAMPGROUND USE IN BOTH PARKS

Camping or parking cars overnight along roadsides or at other undesignated spots is not permitted. Campers must keep their campsites clean. Combustible rubbish should be burned in campfires, and all other garbage and refuse of all kinds should be placed in receptacles provided for the purpose. The drainage or dumping of refuse from any trailer, except in places or receptacles provided for such purpose is prohibited. All campers must carry their waste water to the nearest rest room for disposal. The cleaning of fish or the washing of clothing at campground hydrants is prohibited. Garbage, papers, or refuse of any kind should not be thrown or left on or along roads, in camping or picnic areas, or on any other park land.

Quiet is maintained between the hours of 10 p.m. and 6 a.m. The operation of motor-driven power generators or similar noise-producing motors or machinery is prohibited. The installation of permanent camping facilities by visitors is also prohibited. Campers should not leave their camps unattended for more than 48 hours without special permission of the ranger-in-charge, obtained in advance.

Dogs and cats are allowed in the park if they are on leashes or otherwise under physical restrictive control, but not on trails under any circumstances.

In public campgrounds the regular fireplaces constructed for the convenience of visitors must be used. Take only fallen dead trees for fuel. (Cash-and-carry woodyards near some of the large campgrounds sell Presto-logs and split wood.) As previously stated, campfire permits are required for building fires in areas outside designated campgrounds. The reason for this is obvious. The rangers must know where such fires are being built, since they maintain a constant watch over forests of the park and are on 24-hour fire-call duty.

Be sure your campfire is out before you leave it. There should not be one spark visible. Feel the wet ashes and be sure they are cold before you leave. Be equally careful with your cigarettes. Just one cigarette or match, carelessly thrown, can destroy a whole forest. All kinds of fireworks are prohibited.

Like all animals in all National Parks, bears are wild animals. Because of their protected status they have lost their fear of man. While this may make them appear tame, in this state they are actually more dangerous. Troublesome bears are trapped and removed to remote areas of the park, or in extreme cases must be destroyed. In order that visitors may continue to enjoy the sight of bears roaming freely in the Parks, and to avoid personal injury, please follow these suggestions when camping:

1. Keep a clean camp and use a minimum of odorous food. Seal surplus food in clean wrapping material or in airtight containers. Keep your food as cool as possible, but ice chests are generally not bear-proof. A good deodorizer is effective in eliminating food odors from your camp.

2. Food left on tables or stored in a tent in open boxes or food containers is a natural target for bears and an invitation for bear damage. Back-country campers often suspend their supplies between two trees out of a bear's reach.

3. Food should not be stored in vehicles with convertible tops. Properly wrapped or sealed food is normally safe when stored in the trunk of a hard-topped car provided all windows are closed.

4. Burn all garbage and food containers. Do not bury food scraps and containers. In the back-country pack out any noncombustible litter to the nearest trash containers provided. Report all bear damage and injuries to the campground ranger.

PICNIC FACILITIES

Most of the picnic areas in the two parks are supplied with pit toilets, but drinking water is generally not available. Camping is *not* allowed in a picnic area. Since no fireplaces are supplied, fires are not permitted in the picnic areas in either park.

YELLOWSTONE NATIONAL PARK

The following named picnic areas can be found along the various portions of the Park's roads. The numbers within the parentheses indicate *approximate* the number of sites or tables.

Between Mammoth and Norris Junction: Apollinaris Springs (5), Beaver Pond (12), Sheepeater Cliff (3), Upper Gardner River (2), and Winter Creek (6).

Between Norris Junction and Madison Junction: Gibbon Falls (18), Gibbon Meadows (9), and Tuft Cliff (4).

Between Madison Junction and Old Faithful: Firehole (12), Mallard Creek (15), Nez Percé (6), Upper Nez Percé (12), Goose Lake (6), Whiskey Flats (15), and Feather Lake (6). The latter two are located on Fountain Freight Road.

Between Madison Junction and West Entrance: Madison River (4). A 14-site picnic area can be found at Madison Junction, near the Visitor Center.

Between Mammoth and Tower Junction: Hellroaring (4), and Petrified Tree (2).

(*Continued*)

Between Tower Junction and North East Entrance: Lamar (4), Ice Box Canyon (1), Yellowstone River Bridge (6), and Warm Creek (1).

Between Tower Junction and Canyon Junction: Antelope Creek (1), Canyon Junction (2), Dunraven Pass (10), Cascade Meadows (15), and Old Dunraven Road (13).

Between Norris Junction and Canyon Junction: Gibbon River (3), and Virginia Meadows (4).

Between Canyon Junction and Lake Junction: Buffalo Ford (6), Hayden Valley (8), Le Hardy Rapids (5), Sulphur Cauldron (9), and Yellowstone River (10).

Between Fishing Bridge and East Entrance: Cub Creek (12), Lake Eleanor (3), Mary Bay (1), Sedge Bay (3), Steamboat Point (9), and Sylvan Lake (9). An 8-site picnic area is located on Frank Island in Lake Yellowstone.

Between Lake Junction and West Thumb Junction: Bridge Bay Marina (38), Gull Point (9), Pumice Point (9), Sand Bar Reef (3), Sand Point (19), and Scenic Overlook (8).

Between West Thumb Junction and South Entrance: Grant Village (24), and Lewis River (8).

Between West Thumb Junction and Old Faithful: DeLacy Creek (9), Divide (8), Panorama (6), and Spring Creek (10).

GRAND TETON NATIONAL PARK

The following picnic areas are available within the Parks:

Location

> Employee campfire area north of Colter Bay
> Hermitage Point
> Catholic Church Area
> Foot of Hidden Falls
> Schwabacher Landing on Snake River
> Below Snake River Overlook on Snake River
> Old RKO Site on Snake River
> Cottonwood Creek
> String Lake Picnic Area

ACTIVITIES AND SERVICES

Almost every possible tourist service is available to visitors of the Parks, while the recreational activities are varied, but in keeping with the natural surrounding. The activities and services that are available in the two parks are as follows:

YELLOWSTONE NATIONAL PARK

Mail Service. Visitors should have their mail sent to them in care of General Delivery, Yellowstone National Park, Wyoming 83020, at one of these post offices: Mammoth Hot Springs (main); Old Faithful, Wet Thumb, Fishing Bridge, or Canyon (branches). Those stopping at hotels may have their mail sent in care of the Yellowstone Park Company, Yellowstone National Park, Wyoming 83020, with the name of the hotel where they have reservations. Postal drops are at the front desk of the hotels, inns, lodges, and cabin headquarters.

Telegraph and Telephone. Telegrams may be sent from front desks of inns and hotels to any part of the world during daytime hours. You should use Yellowstone Park, Wyoming, as your telegraphic address, and inquire for messages at the main office in the Mammoth Motor Inn.

Notices of undelivered telegrams and urgent messages are posted daily on bulletin boards at ranger stations, visitor centers, post offices, and elsewhere throughout the Park. (This is also true of Grand Teton National Park.)

Long-distance and local (intrapark) telephone calls may be made from booths located throughout the park.

Medical Service. A well-equipped hospital, with staff physicians and nursing staff, is located just west of the Lake Hotel. Physicians on the hospital staff are on call for emergency medical attention at any point in the Park. Registered nurses are stationed in dispensary at West Thumb, Roosevelt Lodge, Canyon Motor Lodge, Mammoth Clinic (adjacent to Post Office), and both Old Faithful Inn and Lodge.

First aid also may be obtained from ranger stations and visitor centers in case of emergency. Fees for hospital, medical, and ambulance services are approved by the National Park Service and are in keeping with standard charges throughout the country.

Religious Services. Church services—Protestant, Roman Catholic, Christian Science, and Latter-day Saints—are conducted in several areas throughout the park on Sunday, many of them in outdoor amphitheaters. Seventh-day Adventist services are held on Saturday. At all accommodation centers, bulletin boards post time and locations of the church services.

The Protestant services are sponsored by the National Council of Churches; the main service is held at the Yellowstone Park interdenominational chapel at Mammoth Hot Springs, where the Park's resident minister is in charge.

Garages, Service Stations. For automobile repairs, garages are located in the Park at Old Faithful, Fishing Bridge, and Gardiner (at north entrance of the Park). Gasoline service stations are found in the Park at Mammoth, Old Faithful, West Thumb, Lake, Fishing Bridge, and Canyon.

Stores and Newsstands. Hamilton Stores, Inc., carrying groceries and drug supplies, clothing, sportswear and camping equipment, refreshments, newspapers and magazines, and other items are located at Mammoth, Old Faithful, West Thumb, Lake, Fishing Bridge, and Canyon. Some stores are open to serve campers as long as travel is permitted. There are newsstands in all hotels and lodges, where curios, souvenirs, newspapers, magazines, etc., may be purchased.

Photographs and Photo Supplies. Haynes, Inc., operates picture shops at Mammoth, Old Faithful, West Thumb, Fishing Bridge, Canyon, Tower Fall, and Roosevelt Lodge and has shops in the hotels and lodges. Winter Address: Haynes Studios, Inc., 801 North Wallace Street, Bozeman, Montana.

Gift Shop. Gift shops are located in the lobbies of the Canyon Village Motor Lodge, Mammoth Motor Inn, Old Faithful Inn, and next to the office of the Old Faithful Campers' Cabins.

Laundry. Self-service laundromats are in the vicinity of Old Faithful Campers' Cabins and Fishing Bridge cabin office. One-day fluff-dry laundry service is available at West Thumb.

Ice. Ice vendors are located near Fishing Bridge, Lake Hotel, Canyon Village Motor Lodge, West Thumb, Mammoth Motor Inn, and Old Faithful Cafeteria.

Barber Shop and Beauty Shop. These services are available at Lake Lodge, Mammoth Motor Inn, Canyon Village Motor Lodge, and both Old Faithful Inn and Lodge.

Auto Rentals. Automobiles may be rented at the transportation desks at Old Faithful Inn, Lake Hotel, and Mammoth Motor Inn. Chauffeured limousines may also be obtained from the transportation desks.

Transportation. The Yellowstone Park Company's big yellow buses are available for travel throughout the Park from mid-May to mid-October. For further details on bus tours, see page 69.

Stagecoach Rides. Stages depart hourly from the horse corral at Roosevelt Lodge for a ride in beautiful Pleasant Valley.

Entertainment. See bulletin boards in the hotels, inns, lodges, and cabins for daily entertainment schedules. Other activities in the Park such as boating, fishing, and hiking are detailed in previous chapters of this book.

196

GRAND TETON NATIONAL PARK

Mail Service. Post offices are at Moose, Moran, Colter Bay Village, and Elk. (All in the state of Wyoming.) Mail may be sent in care of General Delivery to one of the above post offices, or in care of commercial accommodations you reserve.

Telegraph and Telephone. Telegrams may be sent from the Jackson Lake Lodge and from Jackson. Telephone booths are throughout the Park at most commercial accommodations.

Medical Service. There is a registered nurse at Jackson Lake Lodge; doctors and a hospital can be found in Jackson.

Religious Services. The National Council of Churches ministry in the park holds Protestant services at Colter Bay, Jackson Lake Lodge, and Jenny Lake. Latter-day Saints and Roman Catholic services at these same areas. Episcopal Chapel of the Transfiguration, at Moose, and Roman Catholic Chapel of the Sacred Heart, south edge of Jackson Lake, hold their own services.

Service Stations: Jackson Lake Lodge, Colter Bay, Moose and Signal Mountain Lodge. Garages for auto repair, at Jackson.

Stores. You can shop for groceries and film, curios and post cards at Jenny Lake, Signal Mountain Lodge, Colter Bay, and, of course, in Jackson. There are very fine gift shops at Jackson Lake Lodge, Jenny Lake, and Colter Bay Village. There are also barber and beauty shops at the Lodge. Ice is available at Colter Bay and at Moose. You will find good outfitting stores in Jackson for clothing and simple camping equipment. For rental of camping and fishing equipment, or the purchase of same, see the fishing guides in Jackson. Fishing guide and tackle-shop services are also available at Moose and Colter Bay.

Auto Rentals. Automobiles may be rented at Jackson, at Jackson Airport, or at the Jackson Lake Lodge, Jenny Lake Lodge, and Colter Bay Village.

Transportation. Grand Teton Lodge Company buses operate daily between Jackson and Jackson Lake Lodge and also has a scheduled sightseeing tour (see page 90). Buses also operate daily between Grand Teton and Yellowstone Parks. Limousine service is available between airport and Jackson Lake Lodge.

Scenic Flights. The easiest way to see the tops of the rugged Tetons is by a scenic flight. Such flights leave from Jackson Hole Airport, and information on them may be had at airport or at the Jackson Lake Lodge transportation desk.

Hayride and Campfire Snack. An old-fashioned hayride leaves Jackson Lake Lodge and Colter Bay corrals at 6 p.m. every night but Saturday. Before returning at 9, singing cowboys entertain while the guests enjoy a wiener roast by a stream-side campfire site.

Swimming. Lakes and streams are fed by melting snow and glaciers; the water is quite cold. However, certain shallow bays become sufficiently warm in summer so that swimming may be enjoyed. A swimming beach with lifeguards is located at Colter Bay on Jackson Lake. String Lake, located north of Jenny Lake, is also a popular swimming site. Swimming is prohibited in Jenny Lake because of the extremely cold water, and because Jenny Lake, along with Taggart Lake, are the source of several domestic water systems. A large, outdoor heated swimming pool at Jackson Lake Lodge is available to guests and the public from late June to early September. There is also a public pool near the South Entrance to the Park. (There are no swimming locations in Yellowstone National Park.)

Entertainment. One night each week Reg and Gladys Laubin recreate early American Indian dances in spectacular presentations at Jackson Lake Lodge. On other nights there are movies, square dances, concerts, and nature talks at the Lodge. In the town of Jackson you will find many of the West's frontier features still flourishing such as the board walk, the Pink Garter Theater (a melodrama which can be a family affair), and the nightly capers of the Cache Creek Posse. There are also museums featuring relics of early times and exhibits showing frontier life.

PARK CONCESSIONERS' EMPLOYEES

Tourists in both Yellowstone and Grand Teton National Parks are greeted by the cream of our nation's youth. These are the summer concessioners' employees who come from the fifty states and occasionally from a foreign land. Almost all of Yellowstone's three thousand and Teton's seven hundred employees are college students, who have overcome stiff competition for the privilege of summering, with pay, among some of the world's great wonders. They wear identification badges, naming their home campuses.

The employees are housed in dormitories or cabins close to the facilities where they work. Friends assigned to the same locations room together whenever possible. A limited number of accommodations are provided for the married couples. They live by fairly strict rules. Curfew falls at midnight. There are special activities among the workers at each location in the vast Park. Talent shows, basketball, softball, volleyball, picnics and dances—square and round—are presented during the season, often for the enjoyment of the park's guests. Talent is one of the bases for their selection. When off duty, they ride horses, fish, swim and hike—or just laze in the sun at pine-scented altitudes. With minor exceptions, their meals are the same as are offered to the travelers.

Each year as the tourist season draws to a close at Yellowstone National Park, the employees celebrate Christmas four months early, August 25. The day is observed much as the December holiday is with the exchange of gifts, caroling, and religious services. The "savages," as the students are sometimes called, sing the Messiah, hold Christmas programs, plays, and parties. At most locations of the Christian ministry, students studying for the ministry hold services by candlelight and sing traditional Christmas hymns. Tables in park dining rooms are decorated with holly. Hotel lobbies have Christmas trees with popcorn balls and tinsel. Santa Claus and all his reindeer sweep down from the ceiling on cardboard. A little town in the Middle East called Bethlehem is tableaued. And naturally, as these are college students, mistletoe hangs from every doorway.

For nearly every position that is offered, these young people of Yellowstone have come up with nicknames. For instance, a "gearjammer" is a bus driver, and the seasonal park ranger is a "90-day wonder." Cabin girls are "pillow-punchers" and "packrat" is a porter. Laundry workers are "bubble queens," while a "heaver" is a waitress. Dish-washers are "pearl divers," and a lodge hostess is a "song wrangler."

For information on summer employment in the Parks, write to Yellowstone Park Company, Hamilton Stores, Inc., or the Grand Teton Lodge Company—the Parks' three largest concessionaires —at addresses previously given. Position preference goes to the early May and June arrivals. Most employees stay through mid-September.

WHAT TO WEAR

The climate of both Parks is ideal as a summer retreat from hotter sections of the country. Westerly breezes, cooled by lakes and snowfields high on the mountainsides, give them natural air conditioning all through the summer. *Short* rain-showers frequently cool off the sunny afternoons. Yellowstone's highest temperature was an unusual 96° in 1901 at Mammoth Hot Springs. This is greatly contrasted by the 66° below zero recorded on February 9, 1933 at Riverside Station.

Dress is informal at all times in both Parks, with the emphasis on comfort. Days are usually warm, so have lightweight sportswear with you. A sturdy pair of walking shoes will add to your comfort and enjoyment. (Women's ordinary street shoes are not well adapted for these walks.) Also bring boots and heavy denim trousers. In short, plan for an active outdoor life. Night brings cool weather, so warm clothing is desirable. This means medium overcoats, jackets, "windbreakers," or sweaters. In the lodges, jackets and ties are optional, many guests preferring the comfort of lumberjack shirts and slacks.

Be sure to have suntan lotion along. The mountain sun burns fast through the thinner air, if you are not prepared for it. But, with proper care, you can get a beautiful tan in a remarkably short time. Tinted glasses, serviceable gloves, and a pair of binoculars will be found useful. But remember that you can get practically anything you might need at the Hamilton Stores in Yellowstone Park, or in the shops of Jackson.

Mountain Standard Time, adopted in the United States by the railroads since 1883 and approved by Congress in 1918, applies to the entire park. It is one hour later than Pacific, one hour earlier than Central and two hours earlier than Eastern Standard Time.

PUBLICATIONS

The Yellowstone Library and Museum Association (P. O. Box 17, Yellowstone Park, Wyoming 83020) and the Grand Teton Natural History Association (Moose, Wyoming 83012) are non-profit distributing organizations whose purpose is the stimulation of interest in the educational and inspirational aspects of Yellowstone and Grand Teton history and natural history. The Associations cooperate with and are recognized by the United States Department of the Interior and its Bureau, the National Park Service, as essential operating organizations.

As one means of accomplishing their aims the Associations publish reasonably priced books and booklets which are available for purchase by mail through the year or at the visitor centers' and museums' information desks in the Parks during the summer. The following prices include mailing and handling charges. Orders should be accompanied by check or money order payable to either the Yellowstone Library and Museum Association or the Grand Teton Natural History Association. (Postage stamps will not be accepted. Prices subject to change without notice.)

The available publications are listed as their subject matter appears in this book.

Chapter 1

Yellowstone National Park, Park brochure—Free*
Grand Teton National Park, Park brochure—Free**
The Bannock Indian Trail, A. L. Haynes—40¢*
Chief Joseph's People and Their War, Alvin M. Jossephy—40¢*
The Yellowstone National Park, Hiram M. Chittenden—$2.20 *
Colter's Hell and Jackson's Hole, Merril J. Mattes. A readable history of discovery and exploration of the Yellowstone and Grand Teton regions—$1.10
Campfire Tales of Jackson Hole, edited by Merlin Potts. Stories of early history of Jackson Hole—85¢**
Mountain River Men, Francis Judge—25¢**
From Trapper to Tourist in Jackson Hole, Elizabeth Hayden—$1.60 **

Chapter 2

The Story of Old Faithful Geyser, George D. Marler—50¢*
Yellowstone's Living Geology, W. A. Fischer. Highlights of Yellowstone geology with an interpretation of the 1959 earthquakes and their effects—$1.15 *
Fountain Paint Pots Nature Trail—25¢
Studies of Geysers and Hot Springs Along the Firehole River, George D. Marler—65¢*
Trail Guide to Upper Geyser Basin—10¢

Chapter 3

Haynes Guide to the Yellowstone, J. F. Haynes. A general guide to the Park's roads and geyser locations—$1.70 *

Chapter 4

The Tetons—An Interpretation of a Mountain Landscape, F. M. Fryxell—$2.10 **
Bonney's Guide to Jackson's Hole and Grand Teton National Park, Orrin and Lorraine Bonney—$2.05 **
Jackson Hole, Josephine C. Fabian—$1.10 **

Chapter 5

Yellowstone Back Country, W. Scott Chapman—40¢*
A Climber's Guide to the Teton Range, Leigh Ortenburger—$6.10 **

* Available from the Yellowstone Library and Museum Association only.
** Available from the Grand Teton Natural History Association only.

Chapter 5 (cont.)

Mountain Search and Rescue Operations, Grand Teton Ranger
  Staff—$1.10 **
Jenny Lake Nature Trail—10¢**
Teton Trails, Bryan Harry. A guide to the hiking and horseback
  trails of Grand Teton National Park—$1.10 **
Field Book: The Teton Range, Orrin and Lorraine Bonney. Guide
  to the climbing routes and back country—$3.60 **
Colter Bay Nature Trail—10¢**

Chapter 6

Plants of Yellowstone National Park, W. B. MacDougall & H. A.
  Baggley—$2.70
Trees and Flowering Shrubs of Yellowstone and Grand Teton,
  R. J. Shaw—$1.10
Checklist of Plants in Grand Teton National Park Herbarium—
  Free**

Chapter 7

Checklist of Vertebrates of Grand Teton National Park—Free**
Wildlife of Yellowstone and Grand Teton, Bryan Harry and W. E.
  Dilley—$1.10

Chapter 8

Yellowstone Fishes, James R. Simon—65¢*
A Fishing Guide to Jackson Hole, Harold Hagen—$1.10 **

MAPS

Topographic Map of Grand Teton National Park, U. S. G. S.,
  regular contour—$1.10
Shaded Relief Topographic Map of Grand Teton National Park,
  same as above—$1.10
Topographic Map of Yellowstone National Park, U. S. G. S.,
  regular contour—90¢
Shaded Relief Topographic Map of Yellowstone National Park,
  same as above—90¢
(The above maps mailed folded. Add 30¢ for maps sent in mailing
tube.)

* Available from the Yellowstone Library and Museum Association only.
** Available from the Grand Teton Natural History Association only.

INDEX

The index below covers both Yellowstone and Grand Teton National Parks. To distinguish those entries relating to Grand Teton National Park alone, they are set in italics.

Absaroka Range, 19, 36, 56, 60, 61, 77, 100
Abyss Pool, 51
accommodations, 183-191
Alaska Basin, 106, 107, 108, 111
algae, 21-22, 34, 39, 51, 130
Algal Pool, 51
Alum Creek, 3, 63, 65, 167
Amethyst Mtn., 100, 124
amphibians of the Parks, 152
Amphitheater Lake, 73, 85, 106, 108, 109, 111, 165
animals of the Parks, 131-152
antelope, 80, 137, 138, 140, 146
Antelope Flats, 80, 135, 140, 180
Apollinaris Spring, 44, 45, 120
Arizona Creek, 77, 90, 166
Ranger Station, 90
Artist Point, 63, 64, 65, 69
Artists Paintpots, 47
auto rentals, 196, 197
Avalanche Canyon, 82, 110
Avoca Spring, 51, 53

back-country campsites, 111
etiquette, 112-113
regulations, 112-113
trails, 94-110
badger, 142, 146
bats, 146, 147
Bearpaw Lake, 73, 108, 166, 171
bears, 131, 132, 133, 134-135, 146, 192-193
beaver, 143-144, 146
Beaver Pond, 80, 97, 163
Bechler River, 18, 69, 104, 163
Ranger Station, 69, 105

Beehive Geyser, 52, 53
Berry Creek, 77, 110, 111
Ranger Station, 110
Beryl Spring, 22, 47
Beula Lake, 105, 163
bighorn sheep, 78, 131, 139, 140, 146
Bijah Spring, 44, 45
Bijou Geyser, 51, 53
birds in the Parks, 147-152
Biscuit Basin, 49, 51, 55
bison, 8, 87, 101, 131, 139, 140, 146
Black Canyon, 98
Dragon's Caldron, 15, 30, 62
Pearl Geyser, 51, 53
Pool, 58
Sand Basin, 49, 51, 69
road, 51, 55
Sand Pool, 21, 51
Blacktail Butte, 78, 138
Deer Creek, 68, 97, 98, 164
Deer Plateau, 18, 140
Ponds, 138
Black Warrior Spring, 48
boat cruises, 90, 171, 173
boating in the Parks, 153, 169-173
Bradley Lake, 9, 73, 85, 106, 109, 111, 165, 171
Bridge Bay amphitheater, 61
campground, 59, 60, 189
marina, 59, 60, 158, 160, 169, 170, 171
Bridger, James, 2-3, 8, 44, 63
Brilliant Pool, 51
Broad Creek, 163
Broken Egg Spring, 48
Falls, 77
Buck Mtn., 106, 108, 109

203

204

207

208